Travel
£2

22)

The **AA** POCK[...]

MEXICO

Mexico: Regions and Best places to see

Original text by Fiona Dunlop

Updated by Anto Howard

© Automobile Association Developments Limited 2008
First published 2008

ISBN: 978-0-7495-5525-2

Published by AA Publishing, a trading name of Automobile Association Developments
Limited, whose registered office is Fanum House, Basing View, Basingstoke,
Hampshire RG21 4EA. Registered number 1878835.

Colour separation: Keenes, Andover
Printed and bound in Italy by Printer Trento S.r.l.

Front cover images: (t) AA/C Sawyer; (b) AA/P Wilson
Back cover image: AA/L Dunmire

A03404

Maps in this title produced from mapping © MAIRDUMONT / Falk Verlag 2007
Mapping data © Footprint Handbooks Limited 2004
Transport map © Communicarta Ltd, UK

About this book

Symbols are used to denote the following categories:

➕ map reference

✉ address or location

☎ telephone number

🕐 opening times

✋ admission charge

🍴 restaurant or café on premises or nearby

🚇 nearest underground train station

🚌 nearest bus/tram route

🚉 nearest overground train station

🚢 nearest ferry stop

✈ nearest airport

❓ other practical information

ℹ tourist information office

➤ indicates the page where you will find a fuller description

This book is divided into four sections.

Planning pages 6–19
Before you go; Getting there; Getting around; Being there

Best places to see pages 20–41
The unmissable highlights of any visit to Mexico

Exploring pages 42–121
The best places to visit in Mexico, organized by area

Maps pages 125–144
All map references are to the atlas section. For example, Palenque has the page number and reference ➕ 133 D5 – indicating the grid square in which it can be found

Contents

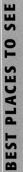

Planning

Before you go

WHEN TO GO

JAN	FEB	MAR	APR	MAY	JUN	JUL	AUG	SEP	OCT	NOV	DEC
19°C	21°C	24°C	26°C	24°C	23°C	23°C	23°C	23°C	21°C	20°C	19°C
66°F	68°F	75°F	79°F	75°F	73°F	73°F	73°F	73°F	70°F	68°F	66°F

High season   Low season

In Mexico, climate depends as much on altitude as it does on latitude or longitude, so it's difficult to make generalizations. The best time to go is in the dry season, between October and April, but even in the "rainy season" the rains usually only fall for an hour or two every day. In the northern states it tends to stay relatively dry year round. The highlands, including Mexico City, are usually mild, but with sharp temperature differences between day and night.

August is vacation time for Mexicans and rooms can be scarce in some of the more popular resorts. Día de los Muertos (Day of the Dead) celebrations at the beginning of November are a fun time to see the locals enjoying themselves.

WHAT YOU NEED

			UK	Germany	USA	Netherlands	Spain
●	Required	Some countries require a passport to remain valid for a minimum period (usually at least six months) beyond the date of entry – check before you travel.					
○	Suggested						
▲	Not required						
Passport (or National Identity Card where applicable)			●	●	●	●	●
Visa (regulations can change – check before you travel)			▲	▲	▲	▲	▲
Tourist Card			●	●	●	●	●
Return Ticket			●	●	●	●	●
Health Inoculations			▲	▲	▲	▲	▲
Travel Insurance			○	○	○	○	○
Driving Licence (national)			●	●	●	●	●
Car Insurance Certificate (pay extra daily fee for CDW)			○	○	○	○	○
Car Registration Document			●	●	●	●	●

WEBSITES

www.visitmexico.com
www.mexconnect.com
www.mexonline.com
www.mexicocity.com.mx

www.mexperience.com
www.mexicanwave.com
www.sectur.gob.mx
www.cybercaptive.com

TOURIST OFFICES AT HOME

In the U.K.

Mexican Tourism Board
Wakefield House
41 Trinity Square
London EC3N 4DJ
☎ 020 7488 9392
Information line: 09065 508917
www.mexicotravel.co.uk

In the U.S.A.

Mexican Tourist Board
400 Madison Avenue
Suite 11C
New York
NY 10017
☎ 212/308-2110
www.visitmexico.com

HEALTH INSURANCE

It is essential to take out a reliable travel insurance policy before leaving home as emergency hospital treatment can be very expensive. For minor ailments pharmacists give good advice, or you can contact a local doctor through your hotel.

Mexican dentists have a very good reputation. If you need emergency treatment, ask at your hotel for a recommendation.

TIME DIFFERENCES

GMT
12 noon

Mexico City
6AM

Germany
1PM

USA (NY)
7AM

Netherlands
1PM

Spain
1PM

Mexico has four time zones. Most of the country runs on Central Standard Time (6 hours behind GMT). The northern states of Nayarit, Sinaloa, Sonora and Baja California Sur are on Mountain Standard Time (7 hours behind GMT). Baja California Norte is on Pacific Standard Time (8 hours behind GMT). Quintana Roo (Cancún) is one hour ahead of Central Standard Time. All regions change their clocks in April and October.

NATIONAL HOLIDAYS

Jan 1 *New Year's Day*
Feb 5 *Constitution Day*
Mar 21 *Benito Juárez Day*
Mar/Apr *Easter (Maundy Thursday, Good Friday,*

Easter Sunday)
May 1 *Labor Day*
May 5 *Battle of Puebla*
Sep 16 *Independence Day (starting eve of 15)*

Oct 12 *Columbus Day*
Nov 1 *All Saints' Day*
Nov 2 *Day of the Dead*
Nov 20 *Revolution Day*
Dec 25 *Christmas*

WHAT'S ON WHEN

January Jan 1*: New Year's Day.
Jan 6: Epiphany (Three Kings' Day), celebrated with a special cake.

February Feb 2: Día de la Candelaria.
Feb 5*: Constitution Day.
Shrovetide Carnivals, above all in Veracruz and Mazatlán.

March Mar 21*: Birthday of Benito Juárez.
Mar 21: Spring Equinox festival in Chichén Itzá.
Easter: Palm Sunday*, Maundy Thursday, Good Friday and Easter Sunday are the big days. Taxco and the Sierra Tarahumara see the greatest celebrations. Feria de las Flores (flower festival) in Xochimilco on Easter Sunday.

April San Marcos National Fair in Aguascalientes with *mariachis*, bullfights, rodeos. Late April to early May – varying dates.

May May 1*: Labor Day.
May 5*: Battle of Puebla (best in Puebla itself).
Cancún International Jazz Festival. Varying dates.
Acapulco Music Festival. Varying dates.

June Feast of Corpus Christi in Mexico City. Varying dates.
Jun 29: Tlaquepaque Festival in Guadalajara. *Mariachis*, dances, parades.

July Third and last Mondays in July: Guelaguetza Festival in Oaxaca.
Music and traditional dances by all Oaxaca's indigenous groups.

August Aug 15: Assumption Day. Streets of Huamantla, Tlaxcala are
carpeted with flower-petal designs.
Mexico City Cultural Festival. Varying dates.

September Sep 15, 16*: Independence Day. Military parades and
festivities nationwide.
President's *grito* on Mexico City's Zócalo.
Sep 21: Autumn Equinox Festival at Chichén Itzá.

October Oct 12*: Día de la Raza (Columbus Day).
Mid- to late-Oct: Cervantino Festival in Guanajuato.
Fiestas de Octubre in Guadalajara. Month-long celebrations with dance,
charreadas, food, arts and crafts exhibits.

November Nov 1: Día de Todos los Santos (All Saints'
Day).
Nov 2: Día de los Muertos (Day of the Dead).
Mexico's fusion of pre-Hispanic and Catholic beliefs
comes to the fore. Renowned celebrations at Pátzcuaro,
Mixquic, Milpa Alta, Iguala. American-style Halloween is
now making inroads on Oct 31.
Nov 20*: Day of the Revolution.

December
Dec 12: Festival of the much-revered Virgen de Guadalupe.
Especially celebrated at the Basílica de Guadalupe, Mexico
City.
Dec 25*: Christmas Day.

* National public holidays when banks and administrative
offices close.

Getting there

BY AIR

Mexico City Airport

13km (8 miles) to city center

- 🚇 35–45 minutes
- 🚌 1 hour
- 🚖 1 hour

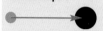
Cancun Airport

16km (10 miles) to city center

- 🚇 N/A
- 🚌 30–45 minutes
- 🚖 30–45 minutes

Visitors flying into Mexico have the choice between Mexico City and international airports at beach resorts such as Cancún, Los Cabos, Acapulco or Puerto Vallarta. Guadalajara and Puebla are increasingly popular alternatives. All have money-changing facilities, taxis, restaurants, and duty-free shops.

BY LAND

Arriving in Mexico overland from the U.S. is a popular and relatively easy option. There are several border crossings, and you can park your car on the U.S. side and walk across for a day visit. You also need Mexican automobile insurance to bring in your own vehicle. Most border crossings have long-distance bus terminals, so you can easily get to your destination from the border. You can also cross by land from Guatemala and Belize.

BY SEA

Cruise ships from all around the world dock in Mexican ports. Destinations such as Acapulco, Cozumel, Ensenada and Puerto Vallarta are popular. Contact a travel agent or website such as www.cruiseweb.com for details and schedules.

Getting around

PUBLIC TRANSPORT

Internal flights Domestic and regional airlines in Mexico are not cheap. Aeromexico and Mexicana have the best schedules and deal with bookings for smaller airlines. Mexicana's Mexipass and Mayapass offer considerable savings if bought in your home country.

Trains Mexico's neglected train service is really only viable for overnight trains from the U.S. border to Mexico City or Guadalajara, or between the two towns. An exception is the spectacular Chihuahua–Pacífico route (► 22–23). South of the capital, trains are slow, dirty and dangerous.

Buses This is the best way of seeing Mexico on a budget. *Primera* (first-class) long-distance bus services offer excellent value. Each large town has a *Central Camionera* (bus station) with private lines operating different schedules and routes. For trips over 5–6 hours or during public holidays, buy your ticket a day or so in advance. Try to avoid buses where your luggage is stowed on the roof.

Ferries The Mar de Cortés has three ferry routes: La Paz–Mazatlán, Santa Rosalía–Guaymas and La Paz–Topolobampo. The Yucatán peninsula has boats from Playa del Carmen to Cozumel, and Puerto Juárez, Punta Sam (car ferry) or Cancún to Isla Mujeres.

Urban transportation Mexico City's metro is excellent and cheap. *Pesero* buses have their destination marked in front, fares are paid to the driver. Elsewhere in Mexico buses and *colectivos* (collective taxis) are easily available, although each city operates different identification systems. Keep small change handy for fares.

FARES AND CONCESSIONS

Students/youths There is little available in the way of reductions for students, as most youth discounts are for Mexican citizens. Children under the age of 12 get reductions on domestic flights and sometimes free beds in their parents' room.

TAXIS

Mexico City and nearby towns use meters. Elsewhere, a flat fare is charged or price negotiated in advance. Airport taxis and *colectivos* are expensive. At night in Mexico City, use radio-taxi services (☎ 55 5519 7690); taxi-muggings are common.

DRIVING

- Mexicans drive on the right side of the road.
- Seat belts are compulsory for front seats.
- Breath-testing is not widespread in Mexico. Due to widespread drinking, as well as hazards such as cattle and *topes* (speed bumps), it is not advisable to drive at night.
- Fuel is Nova (leaded) or Magna Sin (unleaded) and is sold by the liter. Pemex (Mexican fuel) stations are plentiful in central Mexico, but fill up at every opportunity when driving in less populated areas. Payment is in cash. Fuel stations close by 10pm.
- Speed limits are as follows:
  On highways: 110kph (68mph)
  On country roads: 70–80kph (43–50mph)
  In towns: 40–60kph (25–37mph)
- For any breakdown anywhere in Mexico, contact the Angeles Verdes (Green Angels). This unique service is free and provides on-the-spot technical assistance or tows. Every state has an Angeles Verdes Hotline so it is advisable to obtain this before setting off.

CAR RENTAL

International airports have a large choice of car rental companies. Rates vary considerably. In high season (Dec–Mar) it may be cheaper to reserve from home. A credit card is required to make a deposit. Check the car before signing the contract.

Being there

TOURIST OFFICES

Major state tourist offices

SECTUR

Avenida Presidente Masaryk 172,
Bosque de Chapultepec,
11587 Mexico DF
☎ (55) 5250 0123/5250 0151

Baja California Sur

Coordinación General de Turismo,
Carretera Transpeninsular Km 5.5,
Edificio Fidepaz, Apdo Postal 419,
23090 La Paz, Baja California Sur
☎ (612) 124 0100

Chiapas

Secretaría de Desarollo Turístico
Blvd Belisario Domínguez 950,
29000 Tuxtla Gutiérrez, Chiapas
☎ (961) 612 4535/613 39396

Guerrero

Acapulco Convention and Visitors
Bureau
Avenue Costera Miguel Alemán
4455, 39850 Acapulco
☎ (744) 484 2423

Oaxaca

Secretaría de Desarollo Turístico
Avenida Independencia 607,
Centro, 68000 Oaxaca, Oaxaca
☎ (951) 515 0717/514 0570

Yucatán

Departamento de Turismo
Calle 59 No. 514, Centro, 97000
Mérida, Yucatán
☎ (999) 930 3766

MONEY

The monetary unit of Mexico is the peso ($), divided into 100 centavos.
Coins come in10c, 20c, 50c, $1, $2, $5, and $10 denominations. Notes are
in $10, $20, $50, $100, $200, and $500. Major credit cards (particularly
Visa and MasterCard) are accepted at large hotels, restaurants, travel
agents, and stores. Cash machines are widespread, even in small towns.
International airports all have money-changing facilities with good rates.

POSTAL SERVICES

Correos (post offices) are in every town center and open Mon–Fri 8–6.
Overseas mail is slow but generally reliable, and is a better service than
internal post. Post-boxes *(buzón)* are red, but it is safer to post letters at a
post office. For anything urgent or of value, use a courier service.

TIPS/GRATUITIES

Yes ✓   No ✗

Restaurants (if service not included)	✓	10–15%
Cafés/bars	✓	10%
Taxis	✗	
Tour guides	✓	5–10%
Porters	✓	US$1–$2
Chambermaids	✓	US$1 per day
Toilet attendants	✓	$1 (peso)

TELEPHONES

If possible, bring your own international phone card from home with an access number for Mexico. Otherwise, *Ladatel* (long-distance) booths are easily found and operate with phone cards (30 pesos, 50 pesos, 100 pesos) bought at local stores. *Ladatel* offices with operators are also widespread. Avoid making long-distance calls from hotels; taxes increase costs. The country code for Mexico is 52.

International dialing codes
From Mexico to:
U.K.: 00 44
Germany: 00 49
U.S.A. and Canada: 00 1
Netherlands: 00 31
Spain: 00 34

Emergency telephone numbers
Police, fire and ambulance: 080
Green Angels (Tourist patrol): (55) 5250 8221
For other crisis lines, see local phone book.

EMBASSIES AND CONSULATES

U.K. ☎ (55) 5242 8500   Netherlands ☎ (55) 5258 9921

Germany ☎ (55) 5283 2200   Spain ☎ (55) 5280 4383

U.S.A. ☎ (55) 5080 2000

HEALTH ADVICE

Sun advice As in any semitropical country, sunburn is an obvious hazard. Do not sunbathe between noon and 3pm and always use a high-factor sun cream. When visiting archaeological sites, wear a hat.

Drugs Prescription and non-prescription drugs are available from pharmacies *(farmacia)*. Bring a basic first-aid kit: mosquito repellent, antihistamine cream for insect bites, a general antibiotic, pain-relief tablets. Anti-malarial treatment need only be taken if traveling extensively in the rainy season (Jun–Sep) near swamps or lagoons.

Safe water and food Never drink tap water. *Agua purificada* (purified water) or bottled water is always supplied in hotels and bottled water is widely available. Drink plenty of water to avoid dehydration. Moctezuma's Revenge (diarrhea) is a common traveler's complaint in Mexico. Avoid eating salads, uncooked or unpasteurized foods (watch out with ice creams) and drinks with ice, except in decent hotels and restaurants. The liberal use of lime juice apparently acts as a deterrent against bacteria.

PERSONAL SAFETY

Sensible precautions should be taken,
above all in larger cities. Pickpockets operate
in crowded areas such as markets and bus
stations, so do not exhibit jewelry,
cameras, or thick wallets. Do not leave
valuables lying around in your hotel
room; use a safety deposit box.
Muggings are on the increase in
Mexico City (➤ 14, Taxis); only carry
essentials. Elsewhere, avoid taking
solitary walks in remote areas or driving
after dark. If anything is stolen, report it for
insurance purposes.

ELECTRICITY

The power supply is 110 volts. Sockets use two-flat-pin plugs (U.S. style),
so Europeans need an adapter and transformer. Most mid- and upper-
range hotels have universal outlets for shavers.

OPENING HOURS

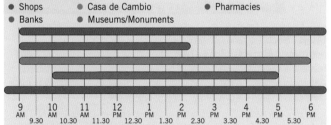

In hotter areas and coastal resorts, shops close at 1 or 2 for lunch,
reopening at 4–5pm and finally closing around 9pm.
Certain banks operate longer hours than above.
Post offices open Monday to Friday 8–6.
Street markets start at 7am.
Museums are generally closed on Mondays, and there are regional
variations to the opening hours.

LANGUAGE

Spanish is the language used throughout Mexico, although in large resorts English is widely spoken. If traveling to smaller places it is essential to know a few basic phrases. Mexican Spanish has slight differences in vocabulary and usage from Castillian Spanish, but otherwise is very similar. Accents change throughout this vast country, and in some areas you will hear local indigenous languages such as Náhuatl, Maya or Zapotec.

Hello! Good morning	*Hola! Buenos días!*	Please/thank you	*Por favor/gracias*
Good afternoon	*Buenas tardes!*	It's a pleasure	*De nada*
Good night	*Buenas noches!*	I don't speak Spanish	*No hablo español*
Goodbye/see you	*Adiós/hasta luego*	Do you speak	*¿Habla inglés?*
Yes/no	*Sí/no*	English?	
Do you have a	*¿Tiene una*	For two nights	*Para dos noches*
single/double room?	*habitación sencilla/*	With fan/air-	*Con ventilador/aire*
	doble?	conditioning	*acondicionado*
With a balcony/sea	*Con balcon/vista*	Is there a swimming-	*¿Hay una alberca?*
view	*al mar*	pool	
How much does it	*¿Cuánto cuesta?/*	Do you take credit	*¿Accepta tarjetas*
cost?	*Cuánta se cobre?*	cards?	*de crédito?*
Very expensive/	*Muy caro/barato/*	Where is the nearest	*Dónde esta el banco*
cheap/too much	*demasiado*	bank?	*mas cerca?*
Can I have the	*El menu/la cuenta,*	A cup of black coffee	*Un café americano/*
menu/bill, please?	*por favor*	with milk	*con leche*
We'll have two beers	*Dos cervezas por*	Fruit juice	*Un jugo de fruta*
please	*favor*	A bottle of red/	*Una botella de vino*
Fizzy mineral water	*Un agua mineral*	white wine	*tinto/blanco*
Where is the bus	*¿Dónde esta el*	How far is the	*¿A qué distancia esta*
station?	*central camionera?*	nearest petrol	*la gasolinera mas*
Straight on/to the	*Todo derecho/a la*	station?	*cerca?*
left/to the right	*izquierda/a la*	How long is the	*¿Cuánto tiempo dura*
	derecha	journey?	*el viaje?*

Best places to see

1 Barranca del Cobre

Rugged canyons, spectacular waterfalls, old mining villages, Jesuit missions, and the Chihuahua-Pacifico railroad are the highlights of the Copper Canyon.

Five times wider and one-and-a-half times deeper than the Grand Canyon, the 35,000sq km (13,510sq miles) Barranca del Cobre is rapidly becoming a major ecotourism destination. It is composed of five adjoining canyons sliced out of the Sierra Madre Occidental, their sculpted ravines offering startling extremes in climate and vegetation. In winter the upper plateau may be blanketed in snow, while on the canyon floors warm, balmy temperatures prevail; in summer the Sierra Tarahumara is refreshingly cooler than oven-like Chihuahua, though rain is abundant.

The most striking access to this region is by rail, through 88 tunnels and over 39 bridges from Los Mochis, near the Mar de Cortés, to Divisadero and Creel, or arriving in the other less scenic direction from Chihuahua. The main town is Creel. Facilities here include day trips on horseback or by van into the surrounding canyons, to Lago Arareco, Cascada de Cusararé, the hot springs of Recohuata or the six-hour ride to Batopilas, a former silver-mining town 2,000m (6,560ft) below on the canyon floor. In the far north are the thundering waters of the Cascada de Basaseáchic, a 246m (807ft) waterfall whose spectacular pine-clad surroundings are now a national park.

The original inhabitants of this region, the Tarahumara, now only number about 50,000. Their geographical isolation has preserved their distinctive traditions that climax during colorful Easter processions.

✚ 127 D6 🚆 Daily 1st- and 2nd-class train leaves Los Mochis at 6am, Chihuahua at 7am ✈ Airports at Los Mochis and Chihuahua ❓ Easter processions and dances peak on Easter Fri

ℹ Libertad 1300, 1st Floor, Edificio Agustín Melgar, Chihuahua

2 Chichén Itzá

This archaeological site is the most popular in the Yucatán peninsula. Two distinct excavated zones present extraordinary and unique structures.

Founded in AD514 by a priest, this ceremonial center experienced two peaks, from 600 to 900, and again from the late 10th century until 1196. Civil wars and cultural stagnation followed before Chichén and other northern Maya civilizations finally collapsed in 1441. When the Spaniards arrived a century later, they named the partially ruined structures according to mere supposition.

At the center of the vast plaza in the northern group rises the striking Pyramid of Kukulkán (El Castillo). Its 365 steps and 52 base panels represent the solar year, and twice a year, at the spring and summer equinoxes, the shadows of the north staircase create a serpentine shape that joins the carved snakes' heads at the bottom. To the northwest is a ball court, the largest yet discovered in Mexico, lined with bas-reliefs of players. Over-shadowing this is the Templo de los Jaguares (Temple of Jaguars), with extensive jaguar and eagle carvings. Beside it stands the macabre Tzompantli (Platform of Skulls), that once displayed the heads of sacrificial victims.

Across the plaza is the richly decorated Templo de los Guerreros (Warriors' Temple) with, at its base, an extensive, roofless colonnade, the Mil Columnas (Thousand Columns). From the platform high above, the entire plaza is surveyed by a much-photographed *chacmool* (seated human figure).

The highlight of the older group is the Caracol (snail), an elevated circular building once used for astronomical observations. Facing it is the ornately decorated Edificio de las Monjas (nunnery) and, between them, the Iglesia (church), crowned by a remarkable roof comb and adorned with masks of the rain god, Chac.

✚ 133 B7 ☎ (985) 851 0137 ③ Site and museum: daily 8–6; services: 8am–10pm 🎫 Expensive; moderate Sun 🍴 Cafeteria ($) 🚌 ADO bus from Mérida, Calle 50 ❓ Sound and light show nightly: 8pm in Spanish; 9pm in English. Spring and fall (autumn) equinox celebrations ℹ️ Tourist information offices in Mérida and Cancún

3 Guanajuato

www.guanajuato.gob.mx

Tumbling down a hillside in central Mexico is this gem of a town. Former silver wealth has left a legacy of superb colonial architecture.

Historically one of Mexico's most important towns, Guanajuato originally earned its status from its rich silver mines, founded in 1546. It never looked back and in 1989 was declared a world heritage site by UNESCO. A network of underground tunnels keeps traffic out of its central plazas and alleys, making it a joy to wander in, though less so to drive in as orientation is not easy.

On a hilltop overlooking the town are the old mines of La Valenciana (one still functions), next to a 1770s church containing three fine baroque altarpieces. Further along the Carretera Panorámica is the Museo de las Momías, another of

Guanajuato's unique sights, containing over 100 mummified bodies retrieved from the local cemetery where they had been impeccably preserved in the mineral-rich soil.

In the town center, the main attraction is the **Alhóndiga de Granaditas,** which houses the regional museum. This imposing building, originally a corn exchange, played a major role in the War of Independence when it became a fortress and later the macabre showcase for the heads of captured rebels. It now exhibits pre-Hispanic objects, altarpieces, religious paintings, and items related to the Independence struggle. A short walk east brings you to the grandiose University, one of the most important in Mexico and, just beyond, the Templo de la Compañia de Jesús, a 1750s church with a remarkable facade. Immediately below is the focal point of town, the lively Jardín de la Unión, backed by the highly decorative Teatro Juárez.

✛ 131 C5 ✈ Flights from Mexico City
🛈 Plaza de la Paz 14 ☎ (473) 732 1982
Alhóndiga de Granaditas
✉ Calle 28 de Septiembre ☎ (473) 732 1112 ⏰ Mon–Sat 10–2, 4–6, Sun 10–3. Closed Dec 25, Jan 1, Easter Sun

4 Huatulco

www.baysofhuatulco.com.mxi

Situated on what was once a deserted coastline, this fledgling resort offers dramatic scenery and excellent services.

Although Huatulco's string of nine bays was spotted by the Spanish conquistadores, they were never exploited as a port. For centuries, this idyllic fishing village slumbered peacefully before being earmarked in the early 1980s by Mexico's resort planners as a follow-up to Cancún. Progress was not always smooth; development suffered from the 1994–5 financial crisis and Hurricane Pauline in 1997. However, unlike other Pacific resorts, planners have learned from their mistakes elsewhere and built an environmentally sensitive resort with low-rise hotels.

Today, Huatulco boasts an international airport, over 20 hotels, a marina, an 18-hole golf course, and three developed beaches at Tangolunda (the most exclusive), Santa Cruz, and Chahue, as well as a lively inland village, La Crucecita, with budget accommodation. Other beaches remain blissfully untouched with, at the most, a few *palapa* restaurants. Between the pockets of hotels are jungle-clad hills and cliffs that are rich in wildlife. Activities include jungle motorbike expeditions, kayaking, snorkeling, and diving around the reefs in Huatulco's clear waters.

Although historical sights are totally absent, Huatulco boasts a modern *zócalo* at the center of La Crucecita. This animated hub is overlooked by a church, **Iglesia de Guadalupe,** worth visiting for its vast contemporary mural of the Virgen de Guadalupe that decorates the entire ceiling vault.

✚ 132 E3 ✈ Flights from Oaxaca, Mexico City

ℹ Santa Cruz, corner Monte Albán, Bahía de Santa Cruz

☎ (958) 581 0176/0177

Iglesia de Guadalupe

✉ Calle Gardenia, La Crucecita ⏰ Daily 9–8 🍴 Cafés and restaurants ($–$$) on plaza

5 Monte Albán

"White Mountain" sits atop a leveled hill above the valley of Oaxaca. Magnificent in scale, layout, and setting, it is an absolute must-see.

Incredible 360-degree views of the barren hills surrounding Monte Albán give a strong sense of proximity to the gods, a fact recognized by the later Mixtecs, who used the abandoned site for offerings and burials between 1350 and the arrival of the Spaniards. The ancient Zapotec site was founded around 500BC and peaked between AD500 and 600 with an estimated population of over 20,000. Like many other Mesoamerican sites, it was abandoned

in the 8th century and, apart from its Mixtec interlude, fell into ruin.

From the site entrance and well-designed museum, a path winds uphill to the corner of the northern pyramid, where the breathtaking Gran Plaza opens up before you. To the left is a ball court, a palace, and small temple platforms, and opposite are three large temple structures. Between them a 300m (985ft) plaza unfolds to the majestic steps of the southern pyramid. Other buildings are aligned down the center, yet the overall sense of space remains absolute from any vantage point.

Behind the northern pyramid are five tombs, the most elaborate being Tomb 104. East of this, near the access path, is Tomb 7, source of the fabulous Mixtec treasures displayed in Oaxaca's museum. On the western flank of the plaza, the Palacio de los Danzantes (Palace of the Dancers) was named after a series of stone slabs carved with dancing figures that stand around its base. There are countless theories about these oddly deformed figures.

✚ 132 D2 ✉ 6km (4 miles) west of Oaxaca ☎ (951) 516 1215 🕐 Daily 8–5 💷 Moderate
🍴 Café ($) on site 🚌 Buses from Oaxaca, Calle Mina 518, every 30 mins 8.30–3.30 ✈ Numerous internal flights to Oaxaca
ℹ Sedetur: Independencia, corner García Vigil, Oaxaca ☎ (951) 516 0123

6 Museo Nacional de Antropología

www.mna.inah.gob.mx

This museum is a must for any visitor to Mexico City, as it houses an exemplary display of the nation's indigenous cultures.

Built in the early 1960s, the Anthropological Museum does full justice to the complexities of

MUSEO NACIONAL DE

Mexico's early civilizations through a dynamic display grouped according to regions. The focal point is a large semi-roofed courtyard fountain; surrounding it are the ground-floor galleries devoted to Mesoamerican artifacts and the upper floor to the rich diversity of surviving traditions among Mexico's indigenous populations. Another attraction is the museum's verdant location in Chapultepec Park, offering a leafy post-museum walk.

The ground-floor galleries start in the right-hand wing and follow a counterclockwise direction around the courtyard. An introduction to world anthropology and ethnology continues with the origins of the Mesoamericans, before moving into pre-Classic civilizations (1700–200BC). Then follow rooms dedicated to Teotihuacán, Tula (the Toltecs), México (the Aztecs), Oaxaca (Mixtecs and Zapotecs), the Gulf of Mexico (Olmecs, Huastecs and Totonacs), Maya, northern desert cultures, and finally Occidente (the western cultures of Nayarit, Jalisco, and Colima). After visiting some of the archaeological sites covered, the museum collection becomes far more relevant and illuminating.

Highlights include the giant Toltec *Atlante* statue in the Sala de Tula, the Aztec Calendar stone in the spectacular Sala México, and a huge Olmec head from San Lorenzo. Other notable exhibits are the superb Olmec *luchador* (wrestler), the Mayan mask of the Sun God, reproductions of Mayan murals from Bonampak, and a reconstruction of King Pakal's tomb from Palenque.

✚ 133 D5 ✉ Paseo de la Reforma, corner Gandhi, Bosque de Chapultepec, Mexico City ☎ (55) 5553 6386/6381
🕐 Tue–Sun 9–7 💵 Moderate 🍴 Café ($) off courtyard
🚇 Chapultepec ❓ Guided tours, audio-guides, bookshop

7 Palenque

Deep in the rainforest of Chiapas stands this superb Maya site, both evocative and historically significant.

Palenque was founded in AD615 by the great Mayan king Pakal, who set out to create a new architectural style. At the center of the main site stands the Palacio (palace), a large complex of courtyards, corridors, and tunnels crowned by a tiered tower that was probably an observatory. The entire structure is decorated with relief carvings, stucco friezes, and carved stelae.

Virtually opposite towers the Templo de las Inscripciones (Temple of Inscriptions), where steep steps rise to a summit temple then descend into the extraordinary tomb of King Pakal. Over 620 hieroglyphic inscriptions (including the date of 692) are surrounded by rich stucco decoration. Pakal's carved sarcophagus remains in the crypt but his fabulous jewelry is now at Mexico City's Anthropological Museum (► 32–33). Temple XIII, immediately to the west, has revealed the entombed body of the Reina Roja (red queen), adorned with fine jade ornaments that are at the site museum.

Across a stream on the hillside is a group of four beautiful temples. Some distance north lies another distinct group where a ball court fronts the Templo del Conde (Count's Temple). From here a path leads along the stream through jungle and past unexcavated structures to the main road and the museum and crafts shop.

➕ 133 D5 ☎ (916) 345 0356/0211 🕐 Daily 8–5
🖐 Moderate 🍴 Cafeteria ($) in museum 🚌 Collectivo bus
to site from Calle Allende, Palenque ✈ Airstrip ❓ As these
ruins are in a remote location, check with your hotel for any
local developments that may affect your safety
ℹ Avenida Juárez, corner Absolo, Palenque

8 Taxco

Taxco boasts a spectacular natural setting high in pine-covered mountains and some impressive colonial extravaganzas.

Taxco, a former staging-post on the royal road south to the port of Acapulco, developed considerably in the 18th century thanks to the enterprising French mining magnate José de la Borda, who left his mark both here and in Cuernavaca. A subsequent long and somnolent period ended in the 1930s when the American William Spratling regenerated the silver industry.

Red-roofed, whitewashed houses tumbling down the slopes line a maze of crooked cobblestoned streets winding uphill from the main road to the Plaza Borda. This social and commercial hub is overshadowed by the magnificent church of **Santa Prisca** (1759), a baroque masterpiece that was entirely financed by Borda. No expense was spared; its ornately carved facade and towers house a dazzling interior lined with 12 gilded altarpieces, oil paintings, and a monumental organ.

On a tiny plaza behind the church, the Museo Guillermo Spratling exhibits pre-Hispanic artifacts and replicas. A few twisting steps downhill from here stands a museum honoring another of Taxco's illustrious foreign residents, the German explorer Baron von Humboldt, who lived here in 1803. His mansion now houses the Museo de Arte Virreinal, a beautifully presented collection of colonial art with some exceptional pieces. There are numerous other fine mansions and churches to be explored, and a lively market area in the streets below Santa Prisca, packed with silver stores, offers the joys of hard bargaining.

Finally, for panoramic views of the town from the summit of Monte Taxco, take the *teleférico* (cable-car) from Los Arcos, located on the main access road.

✚ 131 D6 ❓ Easter Week processions peaking on Easter Fri
ℹ Avenida de los Plateros 1 ☎ (762) 622 6616
Parroquía de Santa Prisca
✉ Plaza Borda ☎ (762) 662 0183 🕐 Mon–Sat 6am–8pm, Sun 5.30am–9pm 🍴 Cafés and restaurants ($) on square

9 Teotihuacán

Long before the Aztecs established their capital in central Mexico, Teotihuacán was the dominant center.

Located an hour's drive from Mexico City, the archaeological site of Teotihuacán ("place of the dead") rises out of dry scrub and cacti. This once magnificent city, that covered over 20sq km (8sq miles) and sustained some 85,000 inhabitants at its zenith, evolved over a period of eight centuries before its destruction around AD750. Controversial 20th-century excavations and restoration of about 80 percent of the structures highlight Teotihuacán's ambitious building, carving, and mural techniques.

The site lies a few degrees off a north–south axis traced by the Avenue of the Dead, that ends at the magnificent Pirámide de la Luna (Pyramid of the Moon). At the southern end is the vast Citadel, a walled quadrangle with the Temple of Quetzalcóatl against the eastern wall. This astonishing stepped construction (around AD200), later built over, honors the plumed serpent (Quetzalcóatl) and the rain god (Tláloc) with 366 stone carvings.

Further north looms the gigantic Pirámide del Sol (Pyramid of the Sun) and, in its southern shadow, a dramatically designed and enlightening new museum displaying priceless exhibits and a huge scale model of the site, crossed by a transparent walkway. At the northwest end of the avenue, flanking another

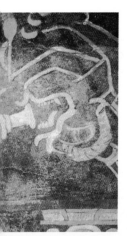

large ceremonial area, stands the extensively restored Palacio de Quetzalpapálotl, part of the priests' residential complex. Here, on an elevated patio, are square columns carved with bird and butterfly designs and remnants of red wall friezes. More patios and lower chambers show depictions of the jaguar god, conch shells, and birds. A climb to the summit of the Pirámide de la Luna offers a final, sweeping view of this once great city.

🔢 131 D6 ☎ (55) 5956 0052 🕐 Daily 7am–6pm
♿ Moderate 🍴 Restaurant ($) opposite the Citadel
🚌 Pirámides' bus from Terminal Tapo 🚇 San Lázaro
❓ Guided tours from Mexico City (Through hotels, travel agents) ℹ️ SECTUR: Avenida Presidente Mazariyk 172, Polanco, Mexico City

10 Xochimilco

Xochimilco is a throwback to the capital's Aztec origins, with its canals and "floating" nursery gardens.

On the far southern edge of Mexico City, weekends are an excuse for feasting on fresh air while cruising the verdant canals of Xochimilco to the insistent tunes of *mariachis*. Brilliantly decorated, pole-propelled *trajineras* (Mexican gondolas), packed with large groups or families, combine with countless flower- and food-sellers in

canoes to create watery traffic jams. But this is Mexico, and chaos is part of the colorful picture.

The tradition of "floating" gardens goes back to the Aztecs, who, due to a shortage of farmland, devised a method of creating islands rooted by willow trees. These *chinampas* were used to grow fruit, vegetables and flowers to supply Tenochtitlán, the capital.

Xochimilco covers an area of 135sq km (52sq miles) that includes the town itself, with its beautiful 16th-century church of San Bernardino de Siena, beside several others, an archaeological museum, and the Parque Ecológico, an extensive area of grasslands, lagoons, and canals. This is an ideal destination for birdwatchers, families or anyone desperate for unpolluted air close to the city center.

Xochimilco's final offering is a fascinating private **museum** housed in an atmospheric 400-year-old hacienda. The vast landscaped grounds are an added draw. Named after its owner, Dolores Olmedo, the museum exhibits an important collection of paintings by Diego Rivera and his wives, Frida Kahlo and Angelina Beloff, as well as pre-Hispanic artifacts (some probably copies) and an impressive collection of folk art.

➕ 131 D6 👑 Moderate 🚈 Tren Ligero: La Noria, from Tasqueña 🚤 Fixed boat prices at Embarcadero ❓ Two-hour tours available (in Spanish) of Parque Ecológico ☎ (55) 5673 8061/7890 or in English through travel agents

Museo Dolores Olmedo Patiño

✉ Avenida México 5843, La Noria ☎ (55) 5555 1221/0891 🕐 Tue–Sun 10–6 except Dec 25, Jan 1 and Easter Sun 🍴 Pleasant open-air café ($)

Exploring

Traveling through Mexico can be a strangely familiar experience because so much of it has clear European and North American influences. But behind this hybrid facade lies the more secret life of the indigenous people, whose ancestors erected the most incredible pyramids and structures.

Traditional crafts reflect the imagination and flair of the Mexicans, whether intricate handweavings, touchingly crude Tarahumara animal carvings, exquisite ceramics and silverware, or tin *milagros* (votive offerings to saints).

Mexico's magnificent Spanish heritage is one of dazzling baroque masterpieces and grid-like urban layouts, with the inevitable *zócalo*, the social crossroads of every town. In contrast, as the northern border draws closer, there is a distinct feel of growing prosperity and increasing Americanization.

Central Mexico

Central Mexico is the volcano-studded heart of the nation's colonial heritage. It was the silver mines of Zacatecas and Guanajuato that financed countless cathedrals in Spain, while a stream of baroque masterpieces was created in a roll-call of towns from Cuernavaca to Querétaro, Morelia, and Puebla.

For today's conquistadores, this is not only one of the most culturally rewarding regions, where interest ranges from local craft specialties to exceptionally designed museums and dramatic archaeological sites, but it also offers spectacular scenery, lakes, forests, and generally cooler temperatures. Political events have marked this region – Morelia was the birthplace of José María Morelos, one of the leaders of the Independence movement, and the state of Morelos was the battleground of Emiliano Zapata, the revolutionary hero.

Mexico City

Vibrant, ever-expanding and highly polluted, Mexico City is the political, cultural and economic heart of the country. Rimmed by volcanoes and lying at an altitude of 2,240m (7,350ft), Mexico's capital now claims over 20 million inhabitants. All of them surrender to the precariousness of living in a city that is sinking into the underground Lago de Texcoco, is plagued by crime and yet survived the terrible earthquake of 1985 with incredible civic solidarity. But despite all its negative factors, no one should pass up on a chance to spend a few days in this stimulating megalopolis.

Mexico City (Ciudad de México) can be divided into three main zones of interest – the Centro Histórico and Alameda area; the Zona Rosa and Chapultepec; and, far to the south, San Angel, Coyoacán, and Xochimilco. From Aztec ruins to impressive colonial edifices interspersed with modern blocks and wide boulevards, it presents strong visual contrasts. And between these facades cruises a stream of traffic, monopolized by the ubiquitous Volkswagen "beetles," the mainstay of the taxi business. In the Centro Histórico, pedicabs have been introduced, offering an alternative, more leisurely form of transport, while the excellent metro system covers the entire city.

Finding your way around can be frustrating, but the streets, alive with color, noise, and activity, more than compensate for this.

ℹ Avenida Presidente Masaryk 172 ☎ (55) 5250 0123/5250 0151

BOSQUE DE CHAPULTEPEC

This extensive park marks the western limits of the city center and is a favorite with some half-a-million city dwellers for weekend walks, picnics, and spontaneous open-air entertainment. Lakes, woods, lawns, museums, an amusement park, a zoo, and restaurants are among its diverse offerings. An entire day can easily be spent here.

Crowning the hill is the 1785 Castillo de Chapultepec, which houses the **Museo Nacional de Historia.** Here, a rather dusty display covers Mexican history, and there are murals and the sumptuous royal apartments of the hapless Emperor Maximilian and his wife, Carlota. Don't miss the sweeping views from the terrace café. The castle is reached by a winding path from the Monumento a los Niños Héroes (Monument to the Young Heroes), at the main park entrance, which passes the snail-like Museo del Caracol (covering Independence and the Revolution) on the way.

The star of Chapultepec is the Museo Nacional de Antropología (➤ 32–33), located on the busy Paseo de la Reforma that slices across the park. Nearby are two major art museums – the Museo de Arte Moderno, and the Museo Rufino Tamayo (which concentrates on temporary exhibitions of contemporary art). Further west lies the Jardín Botánico, boating lakes, restaurants, a high-tech children's museum – **Museo del Papalote** – an amusement park, and the zoo that claims to be the world's oldest, as it existed during Aztec rule.

✠ 134 E1

Museo Nacional de Historia

☎ (55) 5516 2848 🕐 Tue–Sun 10–5 ✋ Inexpensive; free Sun 🍴 Café ($) on premises 🚇 Chapultepec

Museo del Papalote

✉ Avenida Constituyentes, Bosque de Chapultepec ☎ (55) 5237 1781 🕐 Daily 9–1, 2–6 🚇 Constituyentes

CATEDRAL METROPOLITANA

Dominating the Zócalo, Mexico City's main historic square, is this massive cathedral (Latin America's largest), which was begun in 1563, although its baroque facade dates from 1681 and the asymmetrical towers and dome were added in 1813. The walls incorporate stones from the ruins of the Aztec Temple of Quetzalcóatl, but far more visible is the gilded baroque of the Capilla de Los Reyes (Chapel of the Kings) that glows in the gloomy interior. Subsidence is an ongoing problem – note the slope from high altar to the entrance – and metal structural supports are unfortunately highly visible. Next door stands the Churrigueresque-style El Sagrario (The Sacred), with a remarkably ornate facade dating from 1760.

✚ 135 C8 ✉ Zócalo, Centro Histórico 🕐 Daily 7–7 👆 Free 🍴 Cafés ($) on main square 🚇 Zócalo

MUSEO ANAHUACALLI

This outstanding museum is unfortunately located on the far southern edge of Coyoacán and requires some effort to visit. Conceived by the famous muralist and

artist Diego Rivera, it embodies his identification with Mesoamerican culture. The pyramidal lava-stone structure houses his collection of 60,000 pre-Hispanic artifacts and a studio where he worked briefly before his death in 1957, leaving some unfinished paintings. Dark, labyrinthine corridors with onyx windows, stone ceiling mosaics, open terraces, arches, and stepped, altar-like displays all echo pre-Hispanic forms.

🗺 134 F4 ✉ Calle del Museo 150, San Pablo de Tepetlapa ☎ (55) 5617 4310 🕐 Tue–Sun 10–6. Closed Holy Week ✋ Moderate; free Sun 🚇 Taxqueña, then taxi

MUSEO DEL CARMEN

On the edge of the delightful residential area of San Angel, in a cloistered garden, is this former Carmelite monastery, built in 1617 with tiled domes. The attractive, unusual interior encompasses floral friezes, wood and gesso ceiling reliefs, tiles, and frescos. Displayed throughout the former chapels and cells is an important collection of baroque religious art and, in the crypt, a somewhat ghoulish line-up of mummies.

🗺 134 F4 (off map) ✉ Avenida Revolución 4, San Angel ☎ (55) 5616 2816 🕐 Tue–Sun 10–5 ✋ Moderate 🍴 Cafés/restaurants ($–$$) on Plaza San Jacinto 🚌 San Angel *pesero* bus down Insurgentes

a walk through San Angel

A wander through the relaxed neighborhood of San Angel, along tree-lined cobbled streets, takes in ancient churches, museums, and shops.

From the San Angel pesero bus terminal walk up Avenida Revolución to the Museo del Carmen (➤ 49) on your right. After visiting this monument, cross the avenue to the Centro Cultural and walk along Calle Madero to Plaza San Jacinto, lined with shops and restaurants.

On the right-hand side, the 18th-century Casa del Risco offers an unusual ceramic and shell-encrusted fountain, while inside it displays 16th- to 18th-century Mexican and European art. Next door is the Bazar del Sábado, a large

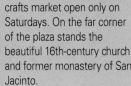

crafts market open only on Saturdays. On the far corner of the plaza stands the beautiful 16th-century church and former monastery of San Jacinto.

Continue along this street, past the crossroads, when it becomes Calle Miguel Hidalgo. At the 17th-century Casa Blanca turn right into Licenciados, following it downhill into Calle Leandro Valle.

These quiet streets offer a classic vision of Mexico City's wealthier residences, often

brightly painted and set behind high walls, in a wide range of architectural styles.

At the main crossroads cross Altavista, passing a beautiful 18th-century hacienda on your left (now the San Angel Inn). Opposite stands the Museo Estudio Diego Rivera.

This blue structure was designed in 1930 for Rivera and includes a smaller, adjoining structure intended for Frida Kahlo. Rivera's studio, where he died in 1957, gives a fascinating insight into his last years.

Walk east down Altavista to Avenida Revolución and the Museo de Arte Carrillo Gil opposite, before returning south to the bus terminal.

Distance About 3km (2 miles)
Time 2–3 hours, depending on stops
Start/end point San Angel bus terminal
Lunch Restaurant Antigua San Angel Inn ($$$)

MUSEO FRANZ MAYER

Opened in 1986 in a superbly restored 16th-century mansion, this museum contains an exceptional collection of 16th- to 19th-century fine and applied arts amassed by German immigrant and construction magnate, Franz Mayer. Influences and contrasts are highlighted between Asian, Middle Eastern, European, and Mexican styles, and priceless exhibits include paintings by Velázquez, Rivera, and Zubarán. Inlaid furniture, tapestries, silver and gold objects, wooden sculptures, glass, and ceramics complete this impressive collection.

➕ 135 B8 ✉ Avenida Hidalgo 45, Colonia Guerrero ☎ (55) 5518 2266 🕐 Tue–Sun 10–5 ✋ Moderate 🍽 Café del Claustro ($) Ⓜ Hidalgo, Bellas Artes

MUSEO FRIDA KAHLO

Deep indigo and red-ochre walls picked out with brilliant green window-frames announce the eclectic and flamboyant tastes of Mexico's foremost woman artist, Frida Kahlo. Located in the pretty tree-lined streets of Coyoacán, where she spent most of her life, her family home reflects her wide-ranging interests and obsessions, and includes some poignant items such as the wheelchair to which she was confined in her last years, her four-poster bed and her last, unfinished painting (a portrait of Stalin). Beside these is a wealth of memorabilia in which Kahlo's husband, the artist Diego Rivera, figures strongly, alongside her collections of masks, Teotihuacán sculptures, ex-votos, glass, lacquerware, and ceramics.

➕ 134 F4 (off map) ✉ Calle Londres 247, Coyoacán ☎ (55) 5554 5999 🕐 Tue–Sun 10–6 👋 Moderate 🍴 Cafés, restaurants ($–$$) on Jardín Centenario 🚇 General Anaya, then taxi

MUSEO NACIONAL DE ANTROPOLOGÍA

Best places to see, pages 32–33.

PALACIO DE BELLAS ARTES

Another of Mexico City's architectural showstoppers presides over the lively park, Alameda Central, on the western edge of the Centro Histórico. The Bellas Artes is a popular cultural center, with excellent temporary exhibitions, a theater where the Ballet Folklórico performs, a bookshop, gift shop, restaurant, and a display of murals by Rivera, Orozco and Siqueiros alongside Tamayo, on the upper floors. Set around a vast marble-lined atrium, the interior is pure art deco, in total contrast to the exuberant domed and colonnaded exterior.

➕ 135 C8 ✉ Corner Avenida Juárez and Eje Central, Centro ☎ (55) 5512 2593 🕐 Palace: daily 10–6; museum: Tue–Sun 10–6 👋 Free 🍴 Café del Palacio ($$) 🚇 Bellas Artes ❓ Ballet Folklórico: Wed, Sun mornings and Sun evenings

PALACIO NACIONAL

Mexico's first parliament is housed within this vast edifice flanking the eastern side of the Zócalo. The 17th-century palace replaced two previous ones, and is still the political powerhouse of Mexico as it holds the offices of the President, the National Archives, and the Federal Treasury. Above the main entrance hangs the symbolic "Freedom Bell" that rang out in the town of Dolores, on September 15, 1810 to announce the fight for Independence. This is rung annually on the eve of Independence Day by the president to teeming masses gathered in the square.

Inside the courtyard a grand staircase leads up past extensive murals by Rivera, a *tour de force* that covers the history of Mexico. It is well worth following a guide to have the endless details explained. A small museum on the second floor is dedicated to Mexico's most revered president Benito Juárez.

✛ 135 C8 (off map) ✉ Zócalo
☎ (55) 9158 1259 🕒 Mon–Sat 9–6, Sun 9–2 ♿ Free, but bring identification
🍴 Cafés ($) on Zócalo 🚇 Zócalo
❓ Military lowering of flag daily before sunset with brass band

TEMPLO MAYOR

On the northeastern corner of the Zócalo is one of the few Aztec sites that remain. When it was completed in 1487, the temple consisted of seven superimposed structures, each one involving a four-day dedication ceremony and several thousand sacrificial victims. It was unearthed by accident in 1978 during construction of the metro. Four years of excavations uncovered hundreds of superb sculptures, housed in a museum behind the site, designed to resemble the temple layout. Visitors can wander through the temple ruins on raised walkways that give close-ups on the altars devoted to Tláloc, god of rain, and Huitzilopochtli, god of war, along with replicas of sculptures. Highly visible is the wall of skulls in front of the museum, while inside, one of the most outstanding exhibits is a huge carved stone disc depicting the dismembered goddess of the moon, Coyolxauhqui.

🚹 135 C8 (off map) ✉ Seminario 8, Centro ☎ (55) 5542 4784 ⏰ Tue–Sun 9–5 🖐 Moderate 🍴 Restaurants ($–$$) in and near Zócalo 🚇 Zócalo

TORRE LATINOAMERICANA

This lofty downtown landmark was the capital's first skyscraper when completed in 1956, but has since been surpassed by others. Towering 139m (456ft), it survived the 1985 earthquake and other tremors due to ingenious anti-seismic foundations that incorporate 361 concrete stilts. Today, it offers the best vantage point for views over the city (on rare, smogless days), particularly breathtaking at night. On the 44th floor is an outdoor viewing deck.

🚹 135 C8 ✉ Corner Avenida Madero and Lázaro Cárdenas ☎ (55) 5512 0844 ⏰ Daily 9.30am–10.30pm 🖐 Moderate 🍴 Cafés and restaurants ($–$$) in Centro Histórico 🚇 Bellas Artes, San Juan de Letrán

XOCHIMILCO

Best places to see, pages 40–41.

More to see in Central Mexico

CHOLULA

Once a major ceremonial town dedicated to Quetzalcóatl, Cholula suffered extensive destruction by Cortés' army on its march to Mexico City. Numerous shrines and churches include the Convento Franciscano (1549) and the 18th-century Capilla Real with its 49 domes. The **Gran Pirámide,** the largest pyramid in the Americas, dominates this otherwise nondescript town. Crowning the summit is the 16th-century Templo de Nuestra

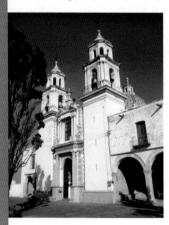

Señora de los Remedios (Temple of Our Lady of Remedies), while below, some 8km (5 miles) of tunnels have revealed extensive remains of murals. A small museum near the tunnel entrance houses copies of the frescos.

✚ 131 D6 ❓ Guides available to explore main tunnel

ℹ Opposite main entrance

Gran Pirámide

✉ Highway 190, Cholula 🕐 Daily 10–5 ✋ Moderate; free Sun 🍴 Restaurant Choloyán ($), Avenida Morelos

CUERNAVACA

Often dubbed the "city of eternal spring," Cuernavaca is a favorite get-away spot for the capital's wealthier inhabitants. Despite a population of over one million, and the largest number of swimming pools per capita in the world, it has a delightful center, and, situated only 65km (40 miles) south of Mexico City, makes an attractive alternative base. Two adjoining plazas form the heart of town, over which looms the **Palacio de Cortés** (1530), a

massive fortress-palace housing a fascinating museum of regional archaeology, colonial history, and the Revolution. There is also a masterful mural by Diego Rivera depicting Spanish oppression of the indigenous peoples.

In front lie the plazas, focal points for a crafts market, promenading, and general festivities. A short walk west up Calle Hidalgo brings you to the magnificent Catedral (1530), built by the Franciscans. Despite being one of Mexico's oldest churches, its interior is strikingly modern. Across Avenida Morelos is the Jardín Borda, a beautiful landscaped garden surrounding a mansion (1783) built by French silver magnate José de la Borda. It was once a favorite retreat for Emperor Maximilian. Historical documents, folk art, and temporary art shows are among the exhibits.

✚ 131 D6

🛈 Avenida Morelos Sur 187, Colonia La Palma ☎ (777) 318 7561

Palacio de Cortés

✉ Avenida Benito Juárez ☎ (777) 312 8171 🕑 Tue–Sun 9–6 💷 Moderate

🍴 Restaurants and cafés ($–$$) on the *zócalo*

GUADALAJARA

Mexico's second-largest city offers a compact historical center and lively traditions from *mariachis* to glass-blowing. The monuments are dotted around four central plazas surrounding the Catedral, a massive edifice that combines numerous architectural styles. Flanking the Plaza de Armas outside is the Palacio Nacional, where Miguel Hidalgo declared an end to slavery, an event captured by Orozco's powerful murals on its walls.

Immediately north is the **Museo Regional de Jalisco** (1701) housed in a former seminary. Exhibits cover pre-Hispanic artifacts, religious and colonial paintings, decorative arts and handicrafts by Jalisco's Huichol and Cora Indians. To the east stands the neo-classical Teatro Delgollado, where Guadalajara's state orchestra and Grupo Folklórico perform. From here, the Plaza Tapatía stretches east to the impressive Instituto Cultural Cabañas. This is the focal point for the city's cultural activities, as well as housing a homage to José Clemente Orozco, the city's renowned 20th-century painter, whose vigorous murals adorn the domed chapel.

Other offerings include a labyrinthine crafts and food market, the Mercado Libertad, and the Plaza de los Mariachis.

Don't miss Tlaquepaque and Tonalá, now engulfed by the urban sprawl. Tlaquepaque makes a colorful outing by bus from the center. Elegant 19th-century mansions converted into restaurants and crafts boutiques radiate from the Jardín Hidalgo and El Parián. Nearby lies Tonalá, with its glass and pottery workshops.

➕ 130 C4

ℹ Monumento Los Arcos, Avenida Vallarta 2641, Zona Minerva ☎ (333) 616 9150 🕒 Mon–Sat 9–7

Museo Regional de Jalisco

✉ Corner Avenida Hidalgo and Liceo ☎ (33) 3614 9957 🕒 Tue–Sat 9–5.30, Sun 9–5 👋 Moderate 🍽 Cafés and restaurants ($) on plazas

GUANAJUATO

Best places to see, pages 26–27.

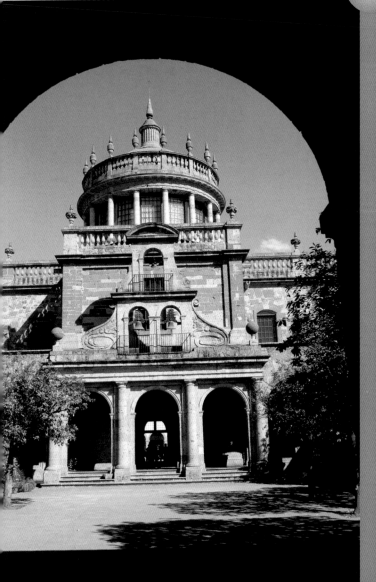

JALAPA (XALAPA)

Blazing sun in the morning and cooler mists in the afternoon characterize Jalapa's picturesque location, high in the coffee-growing hills inland from Veracruz. On the horizon is the Cofre de Perote volcano (4,282m/14,049ft) overlooking this lively university town, with its atmospheric colonial heart of steep, winding streets, gardens, parks, and grandiose administrative buildings. The star sight is the excellent **Museo de Antropología,** an imaginatively designed modern building at the northern end of town. Here sunlit patios and terraced marble halls opening on to a landscaped park display a collection of the pre-Hispanic cultures of the Gulf region. Giant basalt heads from the Olmec center of San Lorenzo vie with the wonderful "smiling" sculptures of the Totonacs at El Tajín and the superb pottery of the northern Huastecs.

✚ 131 D7

🛈 Boulevard Cristóbal Colon 5

☎ (228) 812 8500

Museo de Antropología

✉ Avenida Xalapa, Estado de Veracruz

☎ (228) 815 0920　🕒 Tue–Sun 9–5

✋ Moderate　🍴 Cafeteria ($) in museum

LAGO DE CHAPALA

The warm climate of Mexico's largest natural lake has long attracted a stream of expatriates, from writers such as D. H. Lawrence and Sybille Bedford to today's 6,000 North American retirees. Sleepy

fishing villages stud the lake shore, but the main action is along the northwest shore at Chapala, Ajijic, and Jocotepec. Boat trips visit the two islands of Los Alacranes and Mexcala, the former boasting the lake's most scenic fish restaurants. More authentic in style, and the source of colorful handwoven *serapes* (shawls), is Jocotepec.

➕ 130 C4 ✉ 50km (31 miles) southeast of Guadalajara, 40 mins by car

🍴 Vast choice of cafés and restaurants ($–$$$) along northwest shore

ℹ In Guadalajara (➤ 58)

MORELIA

The uncontested architectural jewel of fertile Michoacán is its capital, Morelia, a dynamic yet compact university town. Although founded in 1541 as Valladolid, it was renamed Morelia at independence to honor Jose María Morelos, a native son and

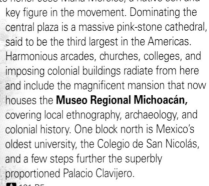

key figure in the movement. Dominating the central plaza is a massive pink-stone cathedral, said to be the third largest in the Americas. Harmonious arcades, churches, colleges, and imposing colonial buildings radiate from here and include the magnificent mansion that now houses the **Museo Regional Michoacán,** covering local ethnography, archaeology, and colonial history. One block north is Mexico's oldest university, the Colegio de San Nicolás, and a few steps further the superbly proportioned Palacio Clavijero.

➕ 131 D5

ℹ Palacio Clavijero, Nigromante 79 ☎ (443) 312 8081

Museo Regional Michoacán

✉ Allende 305, corner of Abasolo ☎ (443) 312 0407

🕐 Tue–Sat 9–7, Sun 9–2. Closed Dec 25, Jan 1, Easter Sun 👜 Moderate 🍴 Cafés and restaurants ($) on square

PÁTZCUARO

Situated beside a tranquil lake, Pátzcuaro is an unusual and delightful little town. Quaint cobbled streets lined with neat whitewashed houses wind uphill from Plaza Vasco de Quiroga and Plaza Gertrudis Bocanegra to reach the Basílica de Nuestra Señora de la Salud. Founded in 1554 but rebuilt in 1883, the church contains a much revered corn-paste statue of the Virgin of Health, and on the eighth day of every month pilgrims flock here with requests. Close by is the **Museo de Artes Populares,** housed in a former college dating from 1540. Inside are displayed Michoacán's rich local crafts, from lacquerware to copper. Downhill from Plaza Gertrudis Bocanegra is the lake. From the main *embarcadero*, boats ferry visitors to the commercialized island of Janitzio. Crowning its hilltop is a gigantic statue of Morelos.

✠ 131 D5

🛈 Plaza Vasco de Quiroga 50, Guion A ☎ (434) 342 1214

Museo de Artes Populares

✉ Enseñanza y Alcantarilla ☎ (434) 342 1029 🕐 Tue–Sat 9–7, Sun 9–3 ✋ Inexpensive 🍴 Cafés and restaurants ($) on main plazas

PUEBLA

Ringed by four volcanoes, including Popocatépetl and Iztacchíhuatl, and less than two hours by road from the capital is Puebla, Mexico's fourth-largest city. Though very industrialized, it is surprisingly easy-going, and offers fabulous examples of baroque architecture, in particular the Templo de Santo Domingo. At the heart of this church is the Capilla del Rosario (1690), the most sumptuous Dominican construction in the world, where gilded and carved stucco blankets the dome and walls as a backdrop to a bejeweled figure of the Virgin.

The 17th-century Ex-Convento de Santa Rosa, now converted into the Museo de las Artesanías, houses the nuns' kitchens where it is said the famed Pueblan *mole* sauce was

invented. Religious art is exhibited at the Ex-Convento de Santa Monica, full of disguised doorways and secret passageways, dating from 1857 when President Juárez closed all religious structures.

Flanking the south of the Zócalo is the vast Catedral, a mixture of various styles due to its prolonged construction between 1575 and 1649. Three blocks southeast is the impressively designed **Museo Amparo,** successfully incorporating high-tech displays of archaeology and viceregal art into a converted 16th-century hospital. Puebla is noted for the Talavera tiles that adorn many facades or domes. Particularly exceptional is the Casa de Alfeñique, home to the Museo Regional, while at Uriarte workshops still make this renowned decorative ceramic.

🔲 131 D6

ℹ️ Avenida 5 Oriente (southern side of Catedral)

☎ (222) 246 2044/1285

Museo Amparo

✉ Calle 2 Sur, corner Avenida 9 Oriente ☎ (222) 229 3850 🕐 Wed–Mon 10–6 🔲 Moderate
🍴 Cafés and restaurants ($) on Zócalo

a drive around Lake Pátzcuaro

Head out of Pátzcuaro on the road to the lake, then follow Highway 14 to Tzintzuntzán, about 20km (12 miles) away.

Above the town is Las Yacatas, a row of stepped, circular pyramids offering sweeping lake views and a small museum. In Tzintzuntzán itself stands the partly ruined 16th-century Templo de San Francisco. Close by are numerous craft outlets for local pottery, woodcarving, and straw figures.

Continue to Quiroga, the largest commercial town on the lake. Turn left at the main square for a short drive to Santa Fe de la Laguna.

It was here in the 1540s that Don Vasco de Quiroga, Michoacán's first bishop, attempted to set up a model

community based on Thomas More's *Utopia*. The 16th-century hospital and chapel still stand and the village square has been completely renovated, together offering an unusual stop.

Continue to skirt the lake through pine forests to the promontory of Chupicaro.

Next stop is San Jerónimo, a sprawling lakeside village jutting out on a small promontory, where activities concentrate on woodcarving and boatbuilding.

Drive on about 15km (9 miles) to the neighboring villages of Puacuaro, Napizaro, and Erongaricuaro.

The pure Purepecha inhabitants of Puacuaro and Napizaro specialize in basket-making. In Erongaricuaro (meaning "look-out tower on the lake") visit the 16th-century Franciscan church and seminary. Handicrafts made here include inlaid furniture, weaving, and embroidery.

The road continues around the lake through San Francisco Uricho, Arocutín, Tocuaro, and San Pedro, before rejoining Highway 14 and returning to Pátzcuaro.

Distance About 65km (40 miles)
Time Allow a leisurely day to include stops
Start/end point Pátzcuaro
Lunch Restaurants ($) at Chupicaro

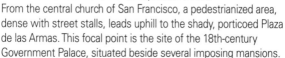

QUERÉTARO

The prosperous, industrial town of Querétaro has a harder edge than its neighbors, yet despite this it is rich in history, with a wealth of baroque architecture and a monumental aqueduct (1735). From the central church of San Francisco, a pedestrianized area, dense with street stalls, leads uphill to the shady, porticoed Plaza de las Armas. This focal point is the site of the 18th-century Government Palace, situated beside several imposing mansions.

Adjoining San Francisco in another former convent is the fabulous Museo Regional, with its renowned collection of viceregal paintings. Southwest from here are Querétaro's two baroque jewels, the Templo de Santa Clara (1633), with walls covered in high-relief altarpieces, and the equally magnificent Templo de Santa Rosa (1752). East of San Francisco stands the church and former Convento de Santa Cruz (1654) that served as a prison for Emperor Maximilian before his execution in 1867.

✚ 131 C5

ℹ Plaza de Armas ☎ (442) 238 5073

SAN MIGUEL DE ALLENDE

This small, picturesque town buzzes with U.S. expatriates, students, and visitors. Reflecting this influx is a plethora of cafés, bars, restaurants, and stores geared to their needs. Rising above lively Plaza Allende are the lofty, neo-gothic spires of the Parroquía (1880), while across a side street stands the 18th-century birthplace of Ignacio Allende, an Independence protagonist. Now the Museo Regional, it illustrates the city's history and archaeology alongside contemporary art. Another impressive 18th-century mansion is the Casa del Mayorazgo; its restored interior now houses an art collection. This artistic theme continues in exhibitions at the Centro Cultural Ignacio Ramírez.

✚ 131 C5

ℹ Plaza Allende ☎ (415) 152 6565

EL TAJÍN

Set in lush, scenic hills are the magnificent ruins of the Totonac civilization (4th–12th centuries). The nearest base is 12km (7 miles) away at the pretty little town of Papantla. El Tajín's main sight is the striking, tiered Pirámide de los Nichos (Pyramid of the Niches), incorporating 365 niches, rising beside numerous other buildings and at least 10 ball courts. The main ball-court walls are carved with fine bas-reliefs depicting players, sacrifices, and *pulque*-drinking. Uphill lies El Tajín Chico, where more structures surround the Edificio de las Columnas, decorated with intricate stone mosaics. At the entrance, outside the excellent modern museum, a 30m (100ft) pole is used by local *voladores* (flying dancers) to re-enact a dangerous but spectacular Totonac ritual.

🚹 131 C7 🖂 Highway 130, Estado de Veracruz (25km/15 miles southeast of Poza Rica) ☎ (784) 842 0026 🕓 Daily 9–6 ✋ Moderate 🍴 Café ($) on site ❓ *Voladores* perform at noon daily

TAXCO

Best places to see, pages 36–37.

TEOTIHUACÁN

Best places to see, pages 38–39.

The North and Baja California

La Paz

Northern Mexico is the land of interminable desert rising abruptly into the Sierra Tarahumara and its canyons (▶ 22–23), while the coastlines are washed by the Pacific Ocean, the Mar de Cortés and, to the east, the Gulf of Mexico. Proximity to the U.S. has generated a string of unattractive industrialized border cities, but in the long finger of land known as Baja California lies a tempting variety of landscapes, from scenic sierra to spectacular, often deserted beaches.

From its border town Tijuana to the southern cape is a distance of 1,200km (746 miles), but it is the southern half that offers the most diversity. This is where whale-watching, bird-watching, sport fishing, scuba diving, riding, and trekking take over, backed up by still-fledgling coastal resorts that contrast with remote Jesuit missions in the sierra.

BAHÍA DE LOS ANGELES

This starkly beautiful bay on the Mar de Cortés makes a welcome change from the dry inland desert and is easily reached from the main highway, 68km (42 miles) away. Facilities include an airstrip, several good hotels, RV parks, restaurants, and the Museo Naturaleza y Cultura. On the horizon lies Isla Angel de la Guarda, a large island reserve, while the waters of the bay are alive with dolphins, finback whales, and sea lions. Boat trips can be arranged.

✚ 126 C3

BARRANCA DEL COBRE

Best places to see, pages 22–23.

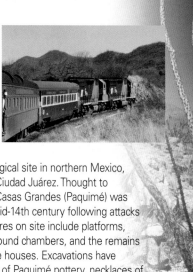

CASAS GRANDES

This is the most important archaeological site in northern Mexico, best reached from Ciudad Juárez. Thought to date from AD1000, Casas Grandes (Paquimé) was abandoned in the mid-14th century following attacks by Apaches. Structures on site include platforms, ball courts, underground chambers, and the remains of three-story adobe houses. Excavations have unearthed rich finds of Paquimé pottery, necklaces of semi-precious stones, and carvings of Quetzalcóatl, some displayed in the museum.

✚ 127 B6 ✉ Zona Arqueológica de Paquimé, Casas Grandes
☎ (636) 692 4140 🕐 Tue–Sun 10–5 👋 Moderate
🍴 Cafeteria ($)

CHIHUAHUA

Capital of Mexico's largest state, Chihuahua means "dry, sandy place" in Náhuatl, yet today this region prospers thanks to cattle ranches, silver, gold and copper mines, and apple orchards. The city is the eastern terminus for the Chihuahua–Pacífico railroad (➤ 22–23), but also offers a number of sights, some linked to Chihuahua's role in the War of Independence and the Revolution. On the central *zócalo* stands the baroque Catedral, and two blocks east is the Palacio Federal, where Miguel Hidalgo was imprisoned in 1811 before his execution. Opposite stands the pink Palacio del Gobierno, originally a Jesuit college, with murals depicting Chihuahua's history.

South of the center are two major museums. The Museo Regional is housed in the Quinta Gameros, a lavishly decorated mansion displaying art nouveau kitsch and a display of Paquimé pottery from Casas Grandes. Four blocks south is the **Museo de la Revolución,** in the mansion where revolutionary leader Pancho Villa lived. Exhibits include photographs, arms, documents, and the black 1922 Dodge peppered with bullet holes in which Villa was assassinated.

✚ 127 C7

ℹ️ Palacio de Gobierno, Plata Baja, Centro ☎ (614) 410 1077

Museo de la Revolución

✉ Calle Décima 3014 ☎ (614) 416 2958 🕐 Tue–Sat 9–1, 3–7, Sun 10–4 💲 Inexpensive

ENSENADA

Just over 100km (62 miles) south of Tijuana lies Ensenada, Baja California's most popular resort, receiving half a million visitors each year. These are mostly Californians on weekend drinking, eating, shopping, and sport fishing sprees, but during the week the town and its bay return to more tranquil fishing and shipping activities. Ultra-fresh seafood is available at the Mercado de Pescas opposite the pier, and local wine can be sampled at the wineries. The largest, **Bodegas Santo Tomás,** offers daily wine tastings in its converted warehouse.

South of town is La Bufadora, a blowhole where wave action produces a dramatic geyser, and the secluded beach of Punta Banda. Nearby are the surfers' favorites of San Miguel, Tres Marías, California, and La Joya.

➕ 126 A1

ℹ️ Tourist and Convention Bureau, Lázaro Cárdenas, corner Miramar

☎ (646) 172 3022

Bodegas Santo Tomás

✉️ Avenida Miramar 666 ☎ (646) 178 3333 🕐 Daily tours at 11, 1, 3

✋ Moderate

GUERRERO NEGRO

Although ostensibly a dull town of endless saltflats, vats, and warehouses, Guerrero Negro is also the entry point to the Laguna Ojo de Liebre (Scammon's Lagoon), a protected national park where gray whales come to breed between December and March. Lookout posts dot the shore and skiffs can be rented at the beach.

➕ 126 C2 ❓ Reserva de la Biosfera El Vizcaino ☎ (615) 157 1777/0177; Eco-Tours Malarrimo ☎ (615) 157 0100

HERMOSILLO

The industrialized city of Hermosillo appears to have little charm, yet its strategic site, 225km (140 miles) south of the border town of Nogales on Highway 15, with access to the beach resorts of Guaymas and Bahía Kino, about 100km (62 miles) west, makes it a good stop-over. The attractive colonial heart centers around the shady Plaza de Zaragoza, flanked by the Catedral and the Palacio de Gobierno. South of here lies the Centro Ecológico de Sonora, a zoo and botanical garden full of indigenous and desert specimens.

On the slopes of the Cerro de la Campaña, a hill overlooking the town, is the **Museo Regional de Sonora** in a converted penitentiary and, further north, the Ciudad Universitario, with its museum of local silk production.

✚ 126 C4

🛈 Palacio de Gobierno, Edificio Norte, Paseo Río Sonora

☎ (662) 172 964

Museo Regional de Sonora

✉ Jesús García Finál, corner Estéban Sarmiento ☎ (662) 217 1241 🕐 Tue–Sat 10–5.30, Sun 9–4 ✋ Moderate; free Sun

LA PAZ

The prosperous capital of Baja California Sur (south Baja), La Paz, lies on a large bay opening on to the Mar de Cortés, an ecologically rich gulf dotted with island nature reserves. Protected to the north by the peninsula of El Mogote, whose shores teem with resort hotels, downtown La Paz looks directly west across the bay. This provides a major natural feature – dramatic sunsets.

La Paz (ironically meaning "peace") suffered a turbulent past, set in motion by Hernán Cortés in 1535. Vicious conflicts with the indigenous inhabitants were exacerbated over the centuries by droughts, famines, smallpox, pirates, American troops during the Texan War and, in 1853, the infamous William Walker, intent on installing slavery. As a result, no indigenous groups survived in Baja. The town's fortunes were revived partly thanks to American sport fishermen, ferry services, the Transpeninsular highway and its free-port status, so that today La Paz boasts one of Mexico's highest per-capita incomes.

The center of La Paz radiates from Plaza Constitución, where the Palacio de Gobierno faces the picturesque 19th-century Catedral de la Señora de la Paz, built on the site of a 1720 mission. Close by is the Teatro de la Ciudad, where modern facilities include art galleries and a library. La Paz's history is covered at the **Museo de Antropología,** where informative displays illustrate Baja geology, the early Pericu, Cochimi and Guaicura inhabitants, and information on the cave paintings near San Ignacio (➤ 81).

The balmy climate, averaging 25°C (77°F), constant breezes, and scenic palm-fringed *malecón* (seafront promenade) make La Paz a relaxing base for exploring the inland sierra, indulging in endless watersports or boat trips, or enjoying the fine white sand of its

beaches. The modernized town center has few historical sights, but Baja is, after all, about the great outdoors.

Although the primary winter (January–March) grounds for humpback whales are around Los Cabos, they sometimes venture into the Bay of La Paz.

Year-round boat trips go to Isla Partida, a seal sanctuary, and the islands of Cerralvo and Espíritu Santo, both nature reserves that offer diving and swimming in the transparent waters of their coves. Sport fishing meanwhile takes advantage of the 850 species of fish in the warm waters of the gulf.

➕ 126 F4

ℹ️ Carretera al Norte km 5.5 ☎ (612) 124 0100. Small office on Tourist Wharf, Paseo Alvaro Obregón 2130 🕐 Mon–Sat

Museo de Antropología

✉️ Calle Altamirano, corner 5 de Mayo ☎ (612) 122 0162 🕐 Mon–Fri 8–6, Sat 9–2 👋 Free 🍴 Cafés and restaurants ($) on Plaza Constitución

a drive through Southern Baja

This drive circles the southern tip of Baja California, passing through dramatic sierra and tiny villages, with a night stop at Los Cabos.

From La Paz drive south on Highway 1 before taking the left fork at San Pedro. From here the road winds up to El Triunfo.

Rich silver veins were discovered here in 1862, leading to a population explosion till the mines closed down in 1926. The town is now virtually a ghost town though small-scale mining has resumed.

Continue 8km (5 miles) to San Antonio, a farming and former silver-mining town, before twisting up into the Sierra El Triunfo. The road descends again to the coast at Los Barriles, renowned for its spectacular winds.

Stop here for a refreshing swim in the Bahía de las Palmas before lunch.

The road skirts the coast before twisting inland and climbing past small villages. About 4km (2.5 miles) beyond Santiago it crosses the Tropic of Cancer, marked by a concrete sphere. At Las Casitas, the road widens to descend to San José del Cabo (► 78–79), an ideal overnight stop. Next morning, head for Cabo San Lucas along the coastal highway and drive to the marina.

Stop here for a glass-bottomed boat trip around the striking rock formation known as El Arco (The Arch).

Drive out of town on Highway 9 to Todos Santos, 80km (50 miles) to the north.

This quiet farming town is attracting a growing community of Americans and a small arts and crafts industry. Beautiful Playa Punta Lobos and Playa San Pedrito are east of town. From here, 80km (50 miles) brings you back to La Paz.

Distance 397km (247 miles)
Time 2 days
Start/end point La Paz ✚ 126 F4
Lunch Hotel Palmas de Cortés ($$) ✉ Conocido en Los Barriles
☎ (624) 141 0050

LORETO

Loreto is a peaceful getaway in a beautiful
setting, backed by the Sierra de la Giganta. The
modest town center claims the well-preserved
Jesuit mission, from where Father Junípero
Serra set out in 1769 to establish a chain of 17
Californian missions. Inside, the **Museo de los
Misiones** gives an informative introduction to
local missionary activities. Around the church is
a pedestrian area leading down to the harbor
and beach where Loreto's few hotels are
located. Activities include tennis at one of the
world's most modern tennis centers, sport
fishing, hiking, and scuba diving, as well as boat
trips to the lovely Isla Coronado. A mega-resort
planned 20km (12 miles) south at Puerto Loreto
has been slow to develop.

✚ 126 E4

Museo de los Misiones

✉ Salvatierra 16 ☎ (613) 135 0005 🕐 Tue–Sun 9–1, 3–6 💲 Inexpensive
🍴 Cafés ($) in nearby plaza

LOS CABOS

At the tip of Baja lie the twin resorts of Cabo San Lucas and
San José del Cabo, 30 minutes apart but with quite distinct
atmospheres. Cabo San Lucas is a boisterous, expensive,

modern golf resort while San José retains a quaint Mexican village atmosphere beneath its touristic veneer. Los Cabos offer luxury hotels, golf courses, sport fishing, surfing, scuba diving at the unique underwater sand cascades, whale-watching, and horse riding in the sierra.

San José dates back to 1730 when its Jesuit mission was founded. Adjacent Paseo Mijáres, with its stone and stucco 19th-century houses, is now the focal point for restaurants, bars, stores, and real-estate agents. At the river estuary, a small **Centro Cultural de Los Cabos** (cultural center) displays arts and crafts, fossils, and reproduction cave-paintings, while next to this is an ecological reserve, home to 200 bird species.

The Baja peninsula ends at El Arco, a massive rock arch that terminates the headland. Boat trips from the marina visit this landmark and El Faro Viejo (Old Lighthouse), which offers panoramic views. Pelicans, seals, sea lions, dolphins, and whales can be seen, while underwater is a paradise for snorkelers and divers.

www.visitloscabos.org

✚ 126 F4

ℹ Hwy 1, Plaza San José, San José del Cabo ☎ (624) 146 9628

Centro Cultural de Los Cabos

✉ Behind Presidente Forum Resort ☎ (866) LOSCABOS 🕐 Tue–Sun 9–5, Wed 9–1 💶 Inexpensive 🍴 Cafés and restaurants ($$) on Paseo Mijáres

MULEGÉ

The sleepy oasis town of Mulegé overlooks the mouth of the
40km (25 miles) Bahía de Concepción, backed by the Sierra de
Santa Lucía. The original settlement was founded beside Baja's
only navigable river, whose water has nourished large groves of
olive trees and date palms. On the hilltop above stands the 1705
Misión de Santa Rosalía, once an open prison and now the Museo
de Mulegé, with an eclectic range of exhibits including old diving
and mining equipment. Low-key Mulegé mainly attracts sport
fishermen, but also offers kayaking upriver or to outlying islands,
scuba diving, and jeep or horse-back trips to see the Cuevas de
San Borjita paintings.

✚ 126 D3 ✋ Moderate ❓ Kayaking and cave-painting tours through Hotel
Hacienda, Calle Romero Rubio, Mulegé ☎ (800) 346 3942

SAN FELIPE

Running from the border town of Mexicali, Highway 5 ends at San
Felipe, a fishing village that has become a resort. The main reason
to come here is for the fishing. San Felipe also attracts beach-
lovers, as its golden sands border the warm Mar de Cortés (as
opposed to the chillier and rougher Pacific). Impressive tides make

the beach south of town popular for dune-buggying, and this is where an increasing number of upscale hotels are appearing.

🕂 126 B2

ℹ️ Mar de Cortés corner Manzanillo ☎ (686) 577 1155

🕐 Tue–Sun 9–2, 4–6

SAN IGNACIO

This attractive oasis town on the edge of the Desierto de Vizcaíno makes a tranquil stop-over as well as being the entry point to Laguna San Ignacio, a major whale-watching spot 70km (43 miles) away. The little town itself features a shady plaza, a beautifully preserved mission church (1786), a small **museum** and date-palm groves planted by the Jesuits. Trips can be arranged to the lagoon during the whale season and all year into the nearby Sierra de San Francisco to see some of the 500 caves painted by the original inhabitants of the area centuries ago (reached by 4WD or horse- or mule-back only).

🕂 126 D3

Museo Pinturas Rupestres

✉️ Misión de San Ignacio

☎ (615) 154 0222

🕐 Mon–Fri 8–3 💰 Moderate

Pacific Mexico

Mexico's oldest beach playgrounds are located along the Pacific coastline between Mazatlán and Acapulco. This is where the country's most dramatic beaches are found, backed by the craggy outline of the Sierra Madre del Sur. Glitzy favorites such as Acapulco and Puerto Vallarta are now joined by Ixtapa-Zihuatanejo, a burgeoning twin resort, and quieter destinations such as San Blas and Barra de Navidad, which offer a more genuine Mexican atmosphere.

Acapulco
de Juárez

Long tracts of coastline remain undeveloped, while short forays can be made inland to hill villages where church bells are the only interruption to a peaceful existence. Watersports are king in these deep blue waters that are sometimes unsuitable for swimming due to their treacherous currents. Acapulco and Puerto Vallarta are the places to go for nightlife, good restaurants, and shopping.

83

ACAPULCO

A stunning sweep of bay heralded Acapulco's rise to fame in the 1950s, a revival of its 16th-century fortunes when it was developed by Cortés and his men as a port. In 1565 the first galleon set sail from Manila in the Philippines (then under Spanish rule) to Acapulco, marking the beginning of a flourishing trade route that saw the wealth of the Orient exchanged with that of Nueva España.

With an international airport and a fast toll road from Mexico City, Acapulco's fortunes are assured. Lining its 11km (7-mile) horseshoe bay are endless high-rise hotels, nightclubs, restaurants, and a string of beaches where watersports and sun-worshipping set the tone. A concrete jungle or a steamy, sybaritic holiday playground? Opinions are divided, but every visitor is at least won over by the stunning scenery.

From the eastern headland of Playa Bruja, the Costera Miguel Alemán sweeps past a succession of facilities that include five golf courses, children's recreation parks, a crafts market, and the San Diego Fort high above the old town, before the bay twists into a peninsula. To the west is the towering cliff of La Quebrada, where daredevil divers plunge into the waves, and beyond this the tranquil beach and Coyuca Lagoon at Pie de la Cuesta. Air-conditioned buses shuttle along the front, making travel easy. Family holidays are much helped by this excellent infrastructure, but remember that Acapulco is an oasis in one of Mexico's poorest states.

✚ 131 F6

ℹ Playa Los Hornos, Costera Miguel Alemán ☎ (74) 844583

Fuerte de San Diego

Overlooking the lively, narrow streets of the old town is this striking stone fort, with panoramic views over the bay and mountains. It was completed in 1617 to protect the thriving port from pirate and buccaneer attacks (including England's notorious Sir Francis Drake). Today, it functions as the Museo Histórico, with interesting historical and ethnographic exhibits.

✉ Calle Morelos and Playa Hornitos ☎ (744) 484 4583
🕐 Tue–Sun 9.30–6.30

Isla la Roqueta

A few hundred yards off the Peninsula de las Playas, this small island, reached by glass-bottomed boats from below the Fuerte de San Diego, offers relaxing respite from the main Costera. Cross the island to reach a small, secluded bay with a restaurant, or climb to the lighthouse. The waters are targeted by scuba divers, who come to see the underwater shrine of La Virgen Sumergida.

✉ Off Peninsula de las Playas

85

Pie de la Cuesta

This long, narrow spit of land separating the Pacific from the mangrove and palm-fringed Laguna Coyuca is a favorite with waterskiers. Sunset fanatics home in on the beach to watch the painted sky from a beach bar hammock and sponsor daredevil locals to pit their strength against the thundering surf. Sadly, in 1997 Hurricane Pauline did extensive damage to this stretch and it will be some time before it regains its idyllic backdrop.

⊠ 11km (7 miles) northwest of Acapulco

La Quebrada

Acapulco's high divers plunge over 40m (130ft) from this cliff into the crashing surf of a narrow cove below. This sight is even more spectacular after sundown, when the last divers carry lighted torches as they plunge. Have dinner or a drink while you witness this carefully timed feat of bravura.

⊠ Hotel Plaza Las Glorias, La Mira
🕐 Daily at 1, 7.15, 8.15, 9.15, 10.15pm 🔅 Inexpensive

More to see in Pacific Mexico

BARRA DE NAVIDAD

This picturesque fishing village developed into an alternative beach resort to soulless Manzanillo, about 60km (37 miles) south. Built on a sandbar next to a large estuary, Barra town offers modest hotels and restaurants, and safe swimming in a scenic setting. Towering above the town is the Grand Bay Hotel, Isla Navidad, with a 27-hole golf course, beach club and a glitzy marina.

✚ 130 D3 ✉ 60km (37 miles) north of Manzanillo
ℹ Jalisco 67 ☎ (315) 355 5100

IXTAPA-ZIHUATANEJO

These twin resort towns are only 6km (4 miles) apart, yet have very different characters. Ixtapa is the modern half, its beachfront lined with high-rise hotels squeezed along the long white-sand Playa del Palmar. The wide bay dotted with tiny islands offers boat trips, windsurfing, waterskiing, and diving, but swimming can be dangerous. When the waves are strong, head for Isla Ixtapa, where a secluded beach fronts a nature reserve. Ixtapa also offers excursions to lagoons, horse riding, sport fishing, golf, and diving.

For some, the former fishing-village setting of Zihuatanejo, with forested headlands plunging into secluded bays, is preferable. Although it is a jazzed-up version of its former self, it offers more atmosphere and older, less pretentious hotels. The least attractive beach, Playa Principal, edges the old town, but beyond a headland

to the southeast are Playa Madera, a family beach with economical hotels; Playa la Ropa, home to chic hotels; and Playa Las Gatas, only accessible by boat.

✚ 130 E4 🚤 Motorboats run all day from Playa Quieta, Ixtapa's northern beach, or sail there with Yates del Sol from Puerto Mio marina ℹ Ixtapa shopping mall ☎ (755) 553 1967

MAZATLÁN

This sprawling resort town is also the largest west coast port between Los Angeles and the Panama Canal, a factor that makes it less commercialized than Mexico's other resorts. Jutting out on a peninsula marked by three hills, its beaches stretch for about 8km (5 miles), lined by a sea-wall promenade, the *malecón*, which ends at El Faro, the headland lighthouse. Behind this hilltop lies the commercial port and old town, while to the far north, Mazatlán's Zona Hotelera monopolizes the seafront.

Despite the influx of tourism, initially attracted by rich sport fishing, Mazatlán still depends on its fishing industry, with tuna-canning factories and shrimp-freezing plants supplied daily by Mexico's largest shrimp fleet. Fish aside, it offers great sports (golf, tennis, riding, watersports), boat trips to two islands with pristine beaches and an atmospheric old town center with a gracious old theater, cathedral, and a small archaeological museum, which displays locally excavated artifacts.

✚ 128 F3

ℹ️ Edificio Banrural, Avenida Camarón Sábalo

☎ (669) 916 5160

PUERTO VALLARTA

Puerto Vallarta (➤ 90–91) is located on Mexico's largest bay, the Bahía de Banderas. It acquired international fame in 1964 when John Huston's film *The Night of the Iguana* hit the screens, with a hot background romance between Richard Burton and Elizabeth Taylor. At that time Vallarta was just a quaint little fishing village with cobbled streets and tile-roofed houses. Today this aspect still exists, as does a moody backdrop of thickly forested hills that sometimes plunge straight into the Pacific, but beyond are high-rise hotels and condos, a marina, hip nightclubs, cosmopolitan restaurants, and a vast array of high-quality stores.

Developments are spreading fast at both ends of the bay, to Mismaloya in the south, where an underwater park lies around the outlying rocks of Los Arcos, and 18km (11 miles) north to the self-contained Nueva Vallarta. Boat trips spirit you to beauty spots such as Boca de Tomatlán, Yelapa, or the Islas Marietas, off Punta Mita. Equally scenic are the roads through the hills, such as to El Tuito; horseback riding or biking are a good alternative to jeeps.

Old Vallarta is still unsurpassed for atmosphere; don't miss the *malecón* and Río Cuale environs. An island at the mouth of this river is home to the **Museo del Cuale,** restaurants, and craft shops, while on its north bank is the *malecón*, town hall and church. The backstreets here are packed with intriguing stores and art galleries. The liveliest town beach, day and night, is Playa Los Muertos, at the southern end of the town center.

✚ 130 C2

🛈 Local 18, Zona Comercial, Hotel Canto del Sol ☎ (322) 224 1175

Museo del Cuale

✉ Isla Cuale 🕔 Tue–Sat 10–3, 4–7, Sun 10–2

SAN BLAS

If you have a good insect repellent and revel in sleepy, unspoiled seaside towns, then this is where to go. Surfing is the number one activity here, closely followed by bird-watching in the mangrove-fringed estuaries and La Tovara lagoon. From November to March over 200 migrating species join the 150 native species. The bay was an important 16th- to 18th-century departure point for Spanish expeditions, and ruins from this period include the old Aduana (Customs House), the hilltop Fuerte de Basilio, and a 1769 church.

✚ 130 B2 ✉ 130km (81 miles) northwest of Puerto Vallarta

🛈 Palacio Municipal ☎ (323) 285 0005

a walk in Puerto Vallarta

This walk winds through atmospheric cobbled streets and leads you across the Río Cuale (▶ 89) to where the Mexican heart still beats.

Start at the church on the main square of Old Vallarta.

The curious crown that tops Nuestra Señora de Guadalupe is a replica of the hapless Empress Carlota's crown. It fell off in a 1994 earthquake, but is now perfectly restored.

Leave the church, turn right into Hidalgo and right again up Iturbide. Climb two steep blocks to Carranza and turn right.

At the end of this street on the left is the Callejón de los Tarques, crossed by the bridge that Elizabeth Taylor and Richard Burton built to connect their two houses. There is a lovely view south from the corner.

Return along Carranza as far as Corona. Turn left and walk two blocks downhill for another superb view, looking north. Walk along Matamoros for five blocks, then turn left at Libertad. This goes over the Río Cuale into Insurgentes. Turn left at Lázaro Cárdenas.

On your left is Santa Cruz (built 1902), a popular neighborhood church.

Continue three blocks further to the Emiliano Zapata market on your right before turning left down Camichín. Climb a few steps at the end to a riverside road. Follow it into Aquiles Serdán and walk straight on, crossing Insurgentes, to Ignacio Vallarta, then turn right. This brings you to steps down on to the Isla Cuale below. Walk west towards the sea.

On your right is the small Museo del Cuale, with an interesting collection of pottery, sculptures, and other artifacts from Jalisco, Narayit, and Colima.

Distance 3km (2 miles)
Time 2 hours
Start point Nuestra Señora de Guadalupe, Old Vallarta
End point Isla Cuale
Lunch Daiquri Dick's Restaurant/Bar ($–$$) ✉ Olas Altas 314
☎ (322) 222 0566
Museo del Cuale
✉ Isla Cuale 🕒 Tue–Sat 10–3, 4–7, Sun 10–2

The South

Indigenous people account for over 75 percent of the population in Southern Mexico, giving this region the look of authenticity. Beyond apparently deserted hills are villages with firmly entrenched customs and craft traditions.

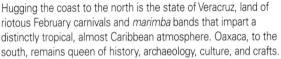

Hugging the coast to the north is the state of Veracruz, land of riotous February carnivals and *marimba* bands that impart a distinctly tropical, almost Caribbean atmosphere. Oaxaca, to the south, remains queen of history, archaeology, culture, and crafts.

East of Veracruz is the oil-rich state of Tabasco, once the heart of Mesoamerica's oldest civilization, the Olmecs, but now clearly a front-runner in fast-developing Mexico.

Furthest south is the troubled state of Chiapas, where indigenous people have suffered at the hands of landowners and economic interests for centuries. This, too, is where high, pine-covered mountains alternate with tropical rainforests that conceal evocative Mayan ruins.

OAXACA

Oaxaca, capital of the state of the same name, is a graceful, small-scale city. Unique, colorful and full of surprises, it is one of Mexico's most relaxed, pleasurable towns. History is omnipresent yet not overpowering, while markets, art galleries, craft shops, cafés, and restaurants make for endless tempting distractions.

At Oaxaca's heart is the magnificent *zócalo*, rimmed by cafés, and a genuine crossroads for anyone in town. Once the center for the Mixtec and Zapotec civilizations, Oaxaca rapidly developed a strong Spanish flavor after it was conquered in 1533. Countless churches (including the masterful baroque Santo Domingo), elegant mansions, government buildings, decorative grille-work, and charming plazas were built, creating a harmonious backdrop for the strikingly proud indigenous population.

In 1987 Oaxaca, together with Monte Albán, a fabulous legacy of the Zapotecs (➤ 30–31) was declared a world heritage site by UNESCO. Excellent services, atmospheric hotels, and a network of craft villages have been organized and made accessible, offering a wide choice of activities to the visitor. The silhouette of Sierra Madre del Sur is a constant reminder of its rural attractions, whether on horseback, bicycle, or by car. However, Oaxaca's charm is best enjoyed on strolls along cobbled streets, past brightly painted houses, peeping into churches or courtyards, checking out shops, or people-watching on the *zócalo*.

Oaxaca endured months of political unrest in 2006, so check first whether it is safe to go (www.travel.state.gov.com).

✚ 132 D2

🛈 García Vigil 517 and Reforma 526

Museo de las Culturas de Oaxaca

Next door to Santo Domingo is the former Dominican monastery that now houses the regional museum, backed by a newly landscaped botanical garden. The rooms and vaulted cloisters of this building display the wealth of archaeological artifacts found in the state. Pride of place goes to the fantastic collection of Mixtec jewelry found in Tomb 7 at Monte Albán, including gold, turquoise, rock-crystal, jade, and silver.

✉ Ex-Convento de Santo Domingo, Alcalá ☎ (951) 516 2991 🕐 Tue–Sun 10–8 💰 Moderate; free Sun

Museo Rufino Tamayo

The late Rufino Tamayo (1899–1991), one of Mexico's foremost 20th-century painters and a native of Oaxaca, spent over 20 years collecting pre-Hispanic antiquities, and this small, select museum is the result. Five color-coordinated rooms display some exceptional pieces, in particular those devoted to the Olmec, Occidente, Totonac, and Maya cultures.

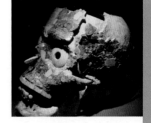

Concerts and art exhibitions are also held here.

✉ Avenida Morelos 503 ☎ (951) 516 4750 🕐 Mon, Wed–Sat 10–2, 4–7, Sun 10–3 💰 Inexpensive

a walk around Oaxaca

This walk through the colonial heart of Oaxaca takes in churches, museums, and the city's inimitable atmosphere.

Start at the Zócalo and head for the Catedral on the north side.

Built in 1533, it contains a bronze altar, antique organ, and, best of all, an elaborate 18th-century baroque facade.

Leave the Catedral, turning sharply right, and walk along Independencia to the pedestrian street of Alcalá. Turn left and walk uphill to the Museo de Arte Contemporáneo. After visiting, continue uphill, turn right along Murguia as far as Cinco de Mayo, then turn left. On your right is the Camino Real Hotel.

This 400-year-old former convent of Santa Catalina, now a national monument, is very picturesque and exudes a distinctive atmosphere.

Continue uphill to Santo Domingo and visit both the church and adjacent museum. On leaving, turn right past the Instituto de Artes Gráficas to the Plazuela del Carmen Alto.

This small plaza is home to a colorful daily market of Oaxacan crafts.

Leave the plaza, turning left onto García Vigil. Continue downhill for four blocks before turning right into Morelos. Two blocks further is the Museo Rufino Tamayo. After visiting, continue another two blocks.

On the left is the Basílica de la Soledad, a late-17th-century church, home to a statue of the town's patron saint and a small museum.

Walk down the steps to Independencia. Turn left and walk four blocks east to the church of San Felipe Neri.

This church (1636) is noted for its fine frescoed walls and ornately gilded altar and nave.

Continue along Independencia to the Zócalo.

Distance 2km (1 mile)
Time 3 hours includ ing stops
Start/end point Zócalo
Lunch Café del Instituto de Artes Gráficas ($) ✉ Alcalá 507
❓ Check www.travel.state.gov.com for the latest on safety in Oaxaca

Templo de Santo Domingo

Started in the late 16th century, this is one of Mexico's finest examples of baroque architecture. Above the main entrance is an extraordinary bas-relief genealogical tree of the family of Domingo de Guzmán, the 13th-century founder of the Dominican order. Beyond this, the soaring ceiling is entirely faced in elaborately gilded and painted stucco, surrounding 36 inset paintings. To the right is the Capilla del Rosario, another magnificent interpretation of Mexican baroque by indigenous artisans.

✉ Alcalá, corner Gurrión 🕐 Mon–Sat 8–7.30, Sun 7–11, 1–7.30 ✋ Free

More to see in the South

HUATULCO
Best places to see, pages 28–29.

MAZUNTE
This delightful, low-key fishing village lies 62km (39 miles) west of Huatulco, between Puerto Angel and Puerto Escondido. A beautiful adjoining beach, San Agustinillo, is popular with Mexicans for long lunches under shady *palapas*. Outlying rocks shelter the beach, making it ideal for those in search of calm waters and fresh seafood. Mazunte itself is home to the world's only turtle research center and the **Museo de la Tortuga,** an impressive modern set-up with turtles representing 9 of the world's 11 types. The wild 15km (9-mile) beach north of here, not accessible by road, sees the arrival of some 200,000 Olive Ridley turtles during their nesting season, from July to December. Mazunte is also home to a local enterprise making natural cosmetics.

✚ 132 E2 (off map)

Museo de la Tortuga

✉ On main road (Mex 200) ☎ (958) 584 3055 🕐 Wed–Sat 10–4.30 ✋ Inexpensive 🍴 Excellent seafood restaurants ($) in Playa San Agustinillo

MITLA

Meaning "place of the dead," this fascinating Zapotec site was occupied between AD400 and 700 but then became solely a ceremonial center. Much of the rich stone-carving was finished by the later Mixtecs, who alternated with the Zapotecs in regional power until the Spanish arrived in 1521. The structures are famed for their complex geometrical stonework, made using an inlay technique. This is particularly well preserved in the Grupo de las Columnas, which contains the masterful Patio de las Grecas. Nearby, another patio structure incorporates two underground cruciform tombs.

The remains of Mixtec murals are displayed in the grounds of the red-domed 16th-century church that rises above the site. Behind it is a large crafts market. The village is dominated by small crafts shops and *mezcal* bars, but don't miss the Frissell Museum, on the plaza at the entrance.

✚ 132 D3 ✉ Highway 190, 45km (28 miles) southeast of Oaxaca ⏰ Daily 8–5 ✋ Inexpensive; free Sun

MONTE ALBÁN

Best places to see, pages 30–31.

PALENQUE

Best places to see, pages 34–35.

PUERTO ANGEL

This charming fishing port, nestling between forested hills, has long been a favorite of those in the know. However, in 1997 Hurricane Pauline caused extensive damage, and although reconstruction was rapid, some scars still remain.

There is little to do here except lap up the sun, lazing on the pretty Playa Panteon and watching diving pelicans, but the slow pace is appealing and the locals are extremely friendly. Ultra-fresh seafood is provided by fishermen who beach their boats or moor at the jetty. A short distance northwest is the hippie beach of Zipolite, where white sands ending in rocky headlands attract backpackers, while surfers revel in the often wild waves. Currents are dangerous and drownings have occurred.

➕ 132 E2 ✉ 83km (52 miles) southeast of Puerto Escondido 🍴 Restaurant Susy ($), Playa del Panteon

PUERTO ESCONDIDO

Of the three beach resorts scattered along the Oaxacan coast, Puerto Escondido takes the middle road between sophisticated Huatulco (➤ 28–29) and relaxed Puerto Angel. Its fishing-village past has receded somewhat with the influx of hotels, restaurants, and shops, but the lovely curved bay is only the beginning; to the east lie palm-fringed Playa Marinero and the surfers' paradise of Playa Zicatela, while to the west is the pretty cove of Puerto Angelito, accessible by boat or road. From Playa Principal a walkway winds around the cliffs, offering sweeping sea views. Nightlife thrives in the form of low-key beach bars.

➕ 132 E2 ✉ 264km (164 miles) south of Oaxaca

ℹ Boulevard Benito Juárez s/n, Fraccionamento Bacocho ☎ (954) 582 0175

SAN CRISTÓBAL DE LAS CASAS

This beautiful but politically troubled town, high in the forested hills east of Tuxtla, remains a prime tourist favorite. Wood smoke fills the air in the narrow cobbled streets, shops offer an amazing array of local crafts, and hotels and restaurants are reasonable. Unfortunately, since the Zapatistas' uprising of 1994 events have proved that little is being done to improve rural conditions.

The main sights in town are the restored cathedral on the main square and, uphill on Avenida General Utrilla, the church of Santo Domingo (1547). Transformed in the 18th century, it presents a lacy, carved facade and an ornate baroque interior. Its terraces throng with an impromptu crafts market daily, while the adjoining monastery houses the **Centro Cultural de los Altos** and the weavers' co-operative, **Sna Jolobil.** The latter displays and sells examples of the skilled techniques still practised by local communities. Handicrafts continue two blocks north at the labyrinthine Mercado. East of here is Na-Bolom, a fascinating institution founded by Frans Blom and his wife Trudy. They both researched and supported local communities, leaving this house as a legacy to anthropologists and writers, who stay here.

San Cristóbal is also the starting point for excursions to local villages. San Juan Chamula, 9km (6 miles) north, has a large Sunday market in front of its extraordinary church. Here the Tzotzils carry on a form of worship that combines Christianity with ancient Mayan spiritual practices. Entry to the church is not allowed during religious ceremonies.

✚ 133 D5　🛈 Delegacion de Turismo, Avenida Miguel Hidalgo 2 ☎ (967) 678 6570/678 1467

Centro Cultural de los Altos

✉ Ex-Convento de Santo Domingo ☎ (967) 81609 🕐 Daily 10–5
✋ Inexpensive; free Sun

Sna Jolobil

✉ Ex-Convento de Santo Domingo ☎ (967) 678 2646 🕐 Mon–Sat 9–2, 4–6
✋ Free

TUXTLA GUTIÉRREZ

Although not an essential attraction in itself, Tuxtla is at the crossroads of several outstanding southern destinations. This modern capital of the state of Chiapas lies in a hot saucer rimmed by hills that rise in the east to San Cristóbal de las Casas. In the town center is the Parque Madero, a cultural complex containing a theater, botanic gardens, and the **Museo Regional,** which has a good display of Olmec and Mayan artifacts. To the south is a unique and enlightened zoo.

Chiapa de Corzo, 17km (10 miles) east on Highway 190, is the state's' first Spanish settlement, dating from 1528. The arcaded main square encloses a fountain structure, La Pila, built to resemble the Spanish crown. One block away is the vast church of Santo Domingo, whose former convent houses the Museo de la Laca (lacquer museum), a local craft specialty. Just behind flows the Río Grijalva. From the *embarcadero* (jetty) boats leave for tours of the Cañon de Sumidero. This canyon, with depths of over 1,000m (3,280ft), can also be viewed from lookout points along a road north of Tuxtla.

✚ 132 D4

ℹ Belisario Domínguez 950 ☎ (961) 602 5298

Museo Regional

✉ Parque Madero ☎ (961) 613 4479 🕐 Tue–Sun 9–4 💵 Inexpensive; free Sun

VERACRUZ

Known above all for its riotous Shrovetide carnival, Veracruz was also the place where Hernán Cortés and his men first landed in 1519. This major port on the Gulf of Mexico later witnessed the arrival of French forces in 1838, and in 1847 was bombarded by the Americans. As a result, many of its monuments date from the late 19th century, with the exception of the beautiful **Fortaleza de San Juan de Ulua,** built in the 16th century and later much extended. Lying north of town in the main port area, the fort's sturdy walls and bastions, which once enclosed a political prison

and presidential palace, now contain a museum.

Life in central Veracruz revolves around the Plaza de Armas, flanked by the Catedral (1734) and the fine Palacio Municipal (1627), where hawkers vie with *marimba* bands long into the steamy night. The aquarium is also exceptional, but for swimming head south to the popular, though dirty, Mocambo beach, near Boca del Río.

✚ 132 C3

Fortaleza de San Juan de Ulua

✉ Islote de San Juan de Ulúa ☎ (228) 938 5151

🕐 Tue–Sun 9–5 🍴 Drinks available 💵 Expensive

VILLAHERMOSA

The modern, oil-rich city of Villahermosa is famed, above all, for its relics of the sophisticated Olmec civilization, Mesoamerica's oldest. A large leisure complex, the Centro de Investigaciones de las Culturas Olmecas (CICOM), includes exceptional Olmec pieces at its Museo de Antropología, but it is at the **Parque Nacional de La Venta** that you will see the impressive giant heads that were hauled here from their original site at La Venta, 95km (59 miles) away. These now sit in a lush, wooded area that also houses an excellent zoo of local Tabasco animals. More insights into local nature lie at Yumka, a well-organized 100ha (247-acre) jungle, savannah, and lagoon refuge for many endangered species.

✠ 132 C4

ℹ Avenue Los Rios y Calle 13 Tabasio 2000, 86035 Villahermosa ☎ (993) 316 3633/316 2889

Parque Nacional de La Venta

✉ Boulevard Adolfo Ruiz Cortines ☎ (933) 314 1652 ⏰ Tue–Sat 9–4.30
✋ Inexpensive; free Sun 🍴 Cafeteria ($)

The Yucatán Peninsula

Jutting out between the Gulf of Mexico and the Caribbean is a flat limestone shelf riddled with underground rivers, caves and *cenotes* (sinkholes). Above ground this peninsula is less than inspiring, consisting mainly of monotonous savannah and low jungle. Yet still it continues to attract charter-loads of visitors.

Mérida

The reason is quite simple; this was the heartland of the great Maya culture and along with Guatemala, claims their most astonishing monuments. Chichén Itzá, Uxmal, Cobá, and Tulum, as well as many lesser-known sites, are a magnet for the historically inclined visitor. And beyond them lie the aquamarine depths of the Caribbean, where underwater life is hard to surpass. Lining the coast is a string of resorts, starting with Cancún, that cater for every touristic and hedonistic whim.

MÉRIDA

The elegant capital of the state of Yucatán makes a relaxed base for exploring major Mayan ruins such as Chichén Itzá (➤ 24–25)

and Uxmal (➤ 120). Mérida has a strong sense of history and culture, much of which has been absorbed from its links with the U.S., Cuba, Europe, and even the Middle East. This unusually cosmopolitan flavor expanded further in the 1950s when direct road and rail links were established with Mexico City.

When the Spaniards arrived in 1542, led by Francisco de Montejo, they used the stones of the declining Mayan city of T'ho to erect their cathedral and administrative structures. But it was not until the late 19th century that Mérida's fortunes really changed. The catalyst was the burgeoning sisal industry, whose prosperous French investors be-queathed an impressive *belle époque* architectural style. Today, many of the earlier colonial buildings around the *zócalo* have been restored, while to the north the tree-lined Paseo de Montejo is home to a string of grandiose edifices that were the residences of the sisal-empire builders. This area is now regarded as "modern" Mérida, characterized by airline offices, large hotels, and nightclubs.

South of the *zócalo*, in the streets surrounding the sprawling market, is a more mundane but authentic quarter, where every-where you will see diminutive Mayan women in embroidered white dresses and older gentlemen in their immaculate white *guayaberas* (tucked shirts).

✚ 133 A6

ℹ Calle 59 No 514 ☎ (999) 930 3760

Casa de Montejo

This is Mérida's first Spanish house, built in 1549 by the conquistador Francisco de Montejo. His descendants lived there

until only a few years ago, but today the mansion more prosaically houses a branch of Banamex (bank). The facade is an outstanding example of the Plateresque style, with sculpted busts and the Montejo coat of arms depicting two soldiers triumphing over the bodies of prostrate Maya.

✉ Plaza Mayor, Calle 63

🕐 Mon–Fri 9–5 ✋ Free

🍴 Cafés and restaurants ($–$$) on square

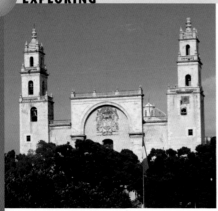

Catedral de San Ildefonso

Built between 1556 and 1599, this is said to be the oldest cathedral on the American continent, although Campeche's inhabitants would not agree. The massive edifice was built with the stones of the dismantled Mayan town of T'ho, but during the 1915 Revolution it was stripped bare. Today's worshippers venerate an impressive 7m-tall (23ft) statue of Christ that dominates the lofty stone interior. Other sights flanking the main square outside are the Palacio Municipal (1735) opposite, and the Palacio de Gobierno (1892) on the northern side, whose interior displays a remarkable series of 27 paintings depicting the complex history of the Maya, Spaniards, and Mexicans.

✉ Plaza Mayor, Calle 60 🕐 Daily 6am–7pm 💷 Free 🍴 Cafés and restaurants ($–$$) on square and along Calle 60

Museo de Antropología e Historia

Located on Mérida's most luxurious avenue, this elaborate 1911 mansion was built for the state governor to rival others belonging to prosperous sisal barons. As a result, the interior Doric columns, marble, chandeliers, and extravagant mouldings somewhat overpower the exhibits. These offer a clear background to the history of the Yucatán, its Mayan sites, and culture. Artifacts include a rare collection of jade offerings recovered from the cenote at Chichén Itzá.

✉ Palacio Canton, Paseo de Montejo 485 ☎ (999) 923 0557 🕐 Tue–Sat 8–8, Sun 8–2 💷 Moderate; free Sun 🍴 Cafés and restaurants ($–$$) along Paseo de Montejo

More to see in the Yucatán Peninsula

CAMPECHE

Founded in the 1540s, Campeche suffered repeated attacks from pirates, and it was not until the erection of thick walls and eight bastions, in the late 17th century that it prospered. There are two excellent museums and several interesting churches, including the Catedral on the main square and the 16th-century church of San Francisco. In the central Baluarte de la Soledad is a superb display of Mayan stelae (carved stone slabs). A **museum** in the hilltop Fuerte de San Miguel has a rare collection of Maya jade and pottery.

✚ 133 B6

ℹ Avenida Ruiz Cortines s/n, Plaza Moch-Couoh ☎ (981) 811 9255

Museo Histórico Fuerte de San Miguel

✉ 4km (2.5 miles) south of Campeche ⏰ Tue–Sun 9–8, Sun 9–1

♨ Inexpensive

CANCÚN

Chosen by computer as the site of Mexico's largest resort in the early 1970s, Cancún attracts over 2.5 million visitors annually to

indulge in powdery white-sand beaches, high-rise hotels, endless entertainment, sports, and shopping. This is hardly the "real" Mexico, but makes an easy base for heading inland or further south along the increasingly developed "Maya Riviera." Most visitors come on package holidays and their 24-hour needs are well catered to. But long before the tourists came, there was a small Mayan settlement here. Its remains are visible at the Ruinas del Rey and at the **Museo Arqueológico.**

✚ 133 A8

🛈 Centro de Convenciones, km 9, Boulevard Kukulcán ☎ (998) 884 6531

Museo Arqueológico

✉ Centro de Convenciones, Km 9, Boulevard Kukulcán A ☎ (998) 883 6671
🕓 Tue–Sun 8–7 👋 Moderate; free Sun

CHICHÉN ITZÁ

Best places to see, pages 24–25.

COBÁ

This lakeside Mayan site remains little visited, despite its significance in the web of *sacbeob* (sacred "white paths") connecting other historic sites. Only a tiny proportion of this enormous city has been excavated, and these ruins are scattered through the jungle, so bring sturdy shoes, water, and insect repellent. Immediately visible is the Grupo de Cobá, whose narrow, steep pyramid rises over 30m (98ft) above the tree-tops to give sweeping views over the lake. A ball court is next on the trail, followed by the Conjunto de las Pinturas (Temple of the Painted Ladies), some carved stelae and altars known as the Grupo Macanxoc. Nearly 3km (2 miles) further on towers 42m-high (138ft) Nohoch Mul, the tallest pyramid in the northern Yucatán peninsula. A strenuous climb is rewarded by a small temple decorated with descending god figures.

✚ 133 B7 ✉ 42km (26 miles) northwest of Tulum ☎ (98) 324634 🕓 Daily 7am–6pm 👋 Moderate; free Sun 🍴 Cafés and restaurants ($)

a drive from Cancún to Cobá

This drive takes you inland from Cancún to the colonial town of Valladolid and the Mayan site of Cobá. A dip in a *cenote* is an option.

Drive west out of Cancún along Avenida López Portillo following signs for Valladolid/Mérida. Avoid the cuota highway (a pricey tollroad, though quicker) and remain on the old Highway 180, which takes you through a string of pretty rural villages.

Traditional Mayan houses are generally elliptical in shape with tightly aligned tree-branch walls and *palapa* (thatched palm-leaf) roofs.

Drive 159km (99 miles) to Valladolid, watching out for the countless topes (speed bumps) that pepper every village. Drive straight into Valladolid's main plaza then follow Calle 41 west for two blocks, where it forks. Go left (Calle 41a) for another three blocks.

In front of you stands the bright yellow San Bernardino de Siena, a 16th-century Franciscan church and monastery. Often targeted by indigenous rebellions, the interior is practically bare.

Continue southwest a few blocks to the Cenote Dzitnup, signposted on the outkirts.

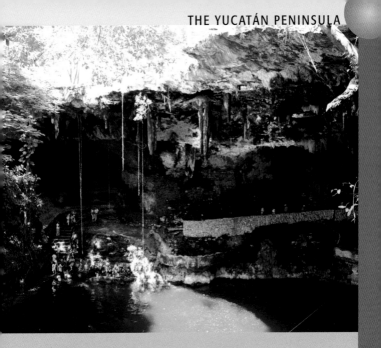

Have a refreshing dip in this beautiful *cenote* before returning to the main plaza. Park, visit the church of San Servacio, shop, then have lunch.

Drive back 28km (17 miles) along Highway 180 to Chemax and turn right to Cobá. Another 30km (19 miles) brings you to this archaeological site (➤ 113). Leave Cobá by following signs to Tulúm, then watch for a turn-off to the left after a few kilometers/miles. This brings you to Tres Reyes and back to Highway 180 or the toll road to Cancún.

Distance 350km (217 miles)
Time 9–10 hours (including stops)
Start/end point Avenida López Portillo, Cancún ✚ 133 A8
Lunch Hotel María de la Luz ($) ✉ Plaza Principal, Valladolid
☎ (985) 856 2071

COZUMEL

Like Cancún, the island of Cozumel is almost entirely geared to the needs of tourists. Cruise ship passengers, scuba divers, and Cancunites all come to taste the delights of the renowned Palankar Reef, one of the world's top diving destinations. Unfortunately the most visited beach, Chankanab, now offers mainly dead coral, although the fish are spectacular. Skilled divers make day trips to some 20 different sites further out. Good swimming beaches dot the southwestern corner of the island, but strong currents make the eastern coast dangerous. In the unspoiled north lies a late Mayan site, **San Gervasio,** with a temple dedicated to Ixchel, goddess of fertility. The main town, San Miguel, is a modernized place, where, again, the flavor of real Mexico is virtually absent.

✚ 133 B8

🛈 Plaza del Sol, in the *zócalo* ☎ (987) 869 0211

San Gervasio

✉ 13km (8 miles) northeast of San Miguel ☎ (987) 800 2215 🕐 Daily 7–5

🚢 Frequent ferries from Playa del Carmen, boat trips from Cancún

GRUTAS DE LOLTÚN

These spectacular underground caves and galleries lie in the heart of the undulating Puuc Hills, south of Mérida. Inhabited over 2,500 years ago, their secret network was also used by rebellious Maya seeking refuge during the mid-19th-century Caste War. Fabulous rock formations, cave paintings, musical stalactites, and the Cathedral, a large chamber that soars over 50m (164ft) high, are all part of this compelling underworld.

✚ 133 B6 (off map) ✉ 115km (71 miles) south of Mérida, 50km (31 miles) east of Uxmal 🕐 Daily guided tours at 9.30, 11, 12.30, 2, 3.30 ✋ Moderate

🍴 Café ($) at entrance

ISLA MUJERES

This delightful little island has a sleepy rhythm of its own. Most streets are of sand, cars are outnumbered by golf-carts and bicycles, and nights are tranquil. It makes an enticing escape from the over-development on Cancún, and as well as good beaches and diving, offers several attractions. The main town and services adjoin Playa Norte, while at the far southern tip is **El Garrafón,** a national park covering part of the Great Mayan Reef. Although the coral is dead, boat trips take snorkelers and divers to better spots further afield.

Half-way down the central lagoon lies Dolphin Discovery, a registered dolphin center, near a turtle farm. A small altar to the fertility goddess Ixchel explains the island's name (island of women); when the Spanish first landed they found numerous crude statues of her. Day trips also go to Isla Contoy, an uninhabited bird sanctuary.

🚩 133 A8

ℹ️ Rueda Medina, opposite jetty ☎ (998) 877 0307

Parque Nacional El Garrafón

✉️ Carretera al Faro ☎ (998) 877 1100 🕐 Daily 8.30–6.30 💲 Expensive 🍴 Snack bar ($) on terrace

PLAYA DEL CARMEN

Once a beach-bum's paradise, this small resort is mushrooming fast. The modern town center is built on a narrow grid of streets bisected by Avenida 5, a favorite promenading and restaurant strip, ending at palm-fringed Caribbean beaches. South of the Cozumel ferry pier is an airstrip and golf course, while north of town hotels are rapidly eating up the shore. Nightlife, eating, and shopping opportunities are plentiful, but there is little else.

➕ 133 B8 ☎ Free info-line 1-800-GO-PLAYA

TULÚM

This dramatic Mayan ruin (AD900–1500) rises perilously on a cliff edge north of a slowly expanding stretch of hotels. Inland lies a typical services town without much beauty but with reasonable prices. However, if you want a few quiet days of sleeping beside the waves, Tulum's beach accommodation is ideal.

The ruins themselves are now fronted by a large shopping plaza from where a tram ferries visitors to the site, although it is within easy walking distance. Sadly, this new structure has taken away much of Tulum's drama, but the Templo de los Frescos is still remarkable for its faded interior murals, the palace for its carved figures, and the Castillo complex for its serpentine columns and sweeping sea views.

➕ 133 B7 ✉ Highway 307 🕐 Daily 8–5 🖐 Moderate; free Sun 🍴 Snack bars ($) in plaza

UXMAL

Uxmal was founded between the 5th and 6th centuries AD and at one point had some 25,000 inhabitants, before being abandoned around 900. It stands on a wide plateau in the Puuc Hills, near several smaller sites of similar style. Outstanding is the Pirámide del Adivino (Magician's Pyramid), an elliptical structure rising over 40m (130ft) high. Immediately to the west stands the Cuadrángulo de las Monjas (The Nuns' Quadrangle), where fine stone inlay typifies the Puuc style. South of here is an elevated complex, the Palacio del Gobernador (Governor's Palace) showing unsurpassed decorative techniques. Beyond is the Casa de las Tortugas (House of the Turtles), the Gran Pirámide (Great Pyramid), and the Casa de la Vieja (Old Lady's House). Visitors with guides can see the last two structures where numerous sculpted phalluses at the Templo de los Falos (Temple of Phalluses) point to a unique cult in Uxmal.

🕂 133 B6 ✉ 78km (48 miles) south of Mérida on Highway 261 🕐 Daily 8–5 🍴 Restaurant ($) in museum complex 🖐 Expensive; moderate Sun ❓ Spectacular sound-and-light show at 7pm in Spanish, 9pm in English

Index

Acknowledgements

The Automobile Association would like to thank the following photographers, companies and picture libraries for their assistance in the preparation of this book.

Abbreviations for the picture credits are as follows – (t) top; (b) bottom; (c) centre; (l) left; (r) right; (AA) AA World Travel Library.

4l Teotihuacán, AA/R Strange; **4c** Lake Arareco, AA/F Dunlop; **4r** Guanajuato, AA/C Sawyer; **5l** Taxco, AA/R Strange; **5r** Guadalupe, AA/R Strange; **6/7** Teotihuacán, AA/R Strange ; **10/1** Pilgrims, AA/R Strange; **12** Cruise Liner, AA/L Dunmire; **13** Bus, AA/C Sawyer; **16** Telephone, AA/L Dunmire; **17** Sign, AA/R Strange; **18** Policeman, AA/C Sawyer; **20/1** Lake Arareco, AA/F Dunlop; **22** Batopilas, AA/ F Dunlop; **22/3** Batopilas, AA/F Dunlop; **24/5t** Chichén Itzá, AA/R Strange; **24/5b** Chichén Itzá, AA/R Strange; **26** Guanajuato, AA/C Sawyer; **26/7** Guanajuato, AA/C Sawyer; **27** Museo de las Momías, AA/R Strange; **28** Beach at Tangolunda in Huatulco, AA/C Sawyer; **28/9** Huatulco, AA/C Sawyer; **30/1** Monte Alban, AA/R Strange; **31** Monte Alban, AA/R Strange; **32/3** Museo Nacional de Antropología, AA/C Sawyer; **34** Palenque, AA/C Sawyer; **34/5** Palenque, AA/C Sawyer; **36/7** Taxco, AA/R Strange; **37** Taxco, AA/R Strange; **38** Teotihuacán, AA/R Strange; **38/9t** Teotihuacán, AA/R Strange; **38/9b** Teotihuacán, AA/R Strange; **40/1** Xochimilco, AA/R Strange; **42/3** Guanajuato, AA/C Sawyer; **45** Children playing, AA/C Sawyer; **46** Palacio Nacional, AA/C Sawyer; **46/7** Bosque de Chapultepec, AA/C Sawyer; **48** Museo Anahuacalli, AA/R Strange; **48/9** Cathedral, AA/C Sawyer; **50** San Angel, AA/C Sawyer; **50/1** San Angel, AA/C Sawyer; **52/3** Museo Frida Kahlo, AA/C Sawyer; **53** Palacio de bellas Artes, AA/P Wilson; **54** Palacio Nacional, AA/C Sawyer; **54/5** Templo Mayor, AA/R Strange; **56** Cholula, AA/R Strange; **56/7** Mariachis, AA/C Sawyer; **58/9** Guadalajara, AA/R Strange; **60** Jalapa, AA/P Wilson; **60/1** Laguna de Chapala, AA/R Strange; **62/3** Patzcuaro, AA/C Sawyer; **63** Puebla, AA/C Sawyer; **64** Patzcuaro, AA/C Sawyer; **64/5** Janitzio, AA/C Sawyer; **66** Queretaro, AA/C Sawyer; **67** El Tajin; AA/R Strange; **68** Restaurant, AA/C Sawyer; **69** Ensenada, AA/L Dunmire; **70** Chihuahua Pacifico railroad, AA/P Wilson; **70/1** Casas Grande, AA/P Wilson; **71** Chihuahua, AA/P Wilson; **72/3** Ensenada, AA/P Wilson; **73** Hermosillo, AA/P Wilson; **74/5** La Paz, AA/L Dunmire; **76** Los Cabos, AA/L Dunmire; **77** Todos Santos, AA/L Dunmire; **78/9t** Loreto, AA/L Dunmire; **78/9b** Loreto, AA/L Dunmire; **80/1t** Museo de Mulege, AA/L Dunmire; **81** San Ignacio, AA/L Dunmire; **82** Food, AA/C Sawyer; **83** Puerto Vallarta, AA/P Wilson; **84** Acapulco, AA/C Sawyer; **84/5** CICI, AA/C Sawyer; **85** Acapulco, AA/C Sawyer; **86/7** La Quebrada, AA/R Strange; **87** View to Isla Ixtapa, AA/ R Strange; **88/9** Puerto Vallarta, AA/R Strange; **90** Puerto Vallarta, AA/R Strange; **91** Puerto Vallarta, AA/R Strange; **92** Blankets for sale, AA/C Sawyer; **93** Local people, AA/C Sawyer; **94** Oaxaca, AA/R Strange; **94/5** Oaxaca, AA/R Strange; **95** Rufino Tamayo Museum, AA/R Strange; **96** Rufino Tamayo Museum, AA/R Strange; **96/7** Oaxaca, AA/C Sawyer; **98/9** Oaxaca, AA; **99** Huatulco, AA/C Sawyer; **100** Mitla, AA/S Watkins; **101** Puerto Escondido, AA/C Sawyer; **102/3** Balloon seller, AA/C Sawyer; **104** Canon de Sumidero, AA/R Strange; **104/5** Musicians, AA/C Sawyer; **106** Villahermosa, AA/R Strange; **107** Fishing Boat, AA/R Strange; **108** Merida, AA/C Sawyer; **108/9t** Merida, AA/R Strange; **108/9b** Casa de Montejo, AA/C Sawyer; **110** Cathedral, AA/C Sawyer; **110/1** Campeche, AA/C Sawyer; **112** Cancun, AA/C Sawyer; **114** Coba, AA/R Strange; **115** Valladolid, AA/C Sawyer; **116/7t** Cozumel, AA/R Strange; **116/7b** Isla Mujeres, AA/C Sawyer; **118** Tulum, AA/P Wilson; **119** Playa del Carmen, AA/C Sawyer; **120** Uxmal, AA/R Strange, **121** Guadalupe, AA/R Strange.

Every effort has been made to trace the copyright holders, and we apologise in advance for any accidental errors. We would be happy to apply the corrections in the following edition of this publication.

Maps

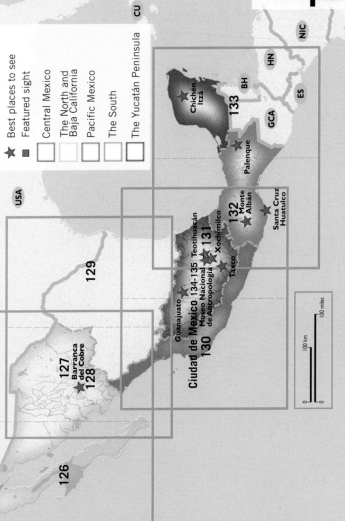

Best places to see
★ Featured sight

- ☐ Central Mexico
- ☐ The North and Baja California
- ☐ Pacific Mexico
- ☐ The South
- ☐ The Yucatán Peninsula

USA

126

127
★ Barranca del Cobre
128

129

130
Ciudad de México 134–135
★ Guanajuato
Museo Nacional de Antropología
131
★ Teotihuacán
★ Xochimilco
★ Taxco

132
★ Monte Albán
★ Santa Cruz Huatulco

133
★ Palenque
★ Chichén Itzá

CU

NIC

HN

BH

ES

GCA

100 km
100 miles

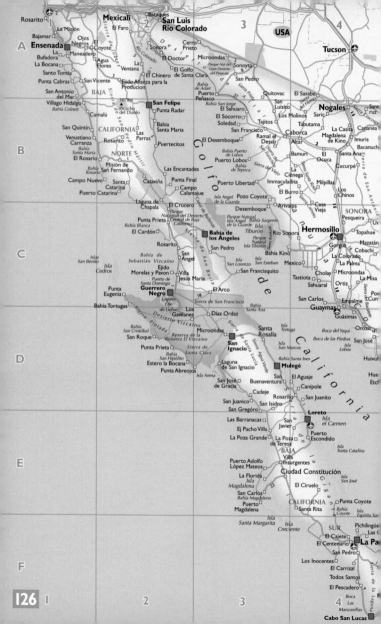

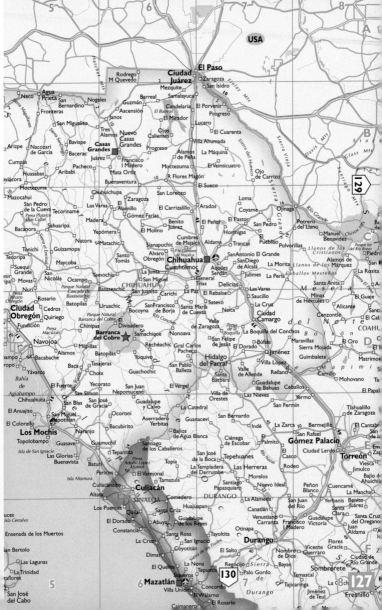

USA

El Paso
Ciudad
Juárez
Zaragoza
San Isidro
Rodrego
M Quevedo
Mezquite
Samalayuca
Barreal
Naco
Agua
Prieta
San
Bernardino
Fronteras
San Miguelito
Nogales
Guzmán
Ascensión
Candelaria
El Porvenir
Progreso
Lucero
El Barreal
El Mirador
Ojos
Calientes
Arizpe
Nacozari
de García
Tres
Alamos
Nuevo
Casas
Grandes
Villa Ahumada
Alamos
de Peña
La Máquina
El Cuarenta
Cumpas
Huasabas
Bavispe
Bacerac
Pacheco
Aribabi
Juárez
Francisco
I Madero
Mata Ortiz
Moctezuma
El Veinticuatro
Ojo
de Carrizo
Buenaventura
Chuhuichupa
Zaragoza
R Flores Magón
El Sueco
Loma
Coyame
Ojinaga
Potrero
del Llano
San Lorenzo
El Carrizalillo
Arados
Mazocahui
San Pedro
de la Cueva
Tecoriname
Las Varas
Alamillo
Gómez Farías
Benito
Juárez
El Peñol
El Pastor
San Pedro
El
Pueblito
Polvorillas
Manuel
Benavides
Bacanora
Sahuaripa
Madera
El Molino
Cumbres
de Majalca
Aldama
Hormigas
Trancas
Llanos de los
Cristianos
Tonichi
Guizamopa
Yepómera
Matachic
Santo
Tomás
Sianapuchic
de Majalca
Chihuahua
SanAntonio El Grande
SanDiego
de Alcalá
La Morita
Llanos de los Márquez
Alamos
de Piedra
Tedoripa
Maycoba
Alvaro
Obregón
Cuauhtémoc
Aquiles
Serdán
Julimes
La Perla
Caballos Mesteños
Santa Anita
Suaqui
Grande
San
Nicolás
Ocampo
Temochic
La Junta
CHIHUAHUA
San Miguel
General
Trias
Delicias
Las Varas
Minas
de Hércules
El Guaje
Nuri
Rosario
Cedros
Basaseachic
San Juanito
Carichi
La Paz
El Rebalse
La Cruz
Naica
Alicante
Cenzontle
Ciudad
Obregón
Quiriego
Uruachic
San Francisco
de Borja
Santa María
de Cuevas
Satevó
Ciudad
Camargo
El Cal
Fundición
Chinipas
Divisadero
Samachique
Rio Conchos
Valle
de Zaragoza
La Boquilla del Conchos
El Oro
Barranca
del Cobre
Rechéachic
Nonoava
Presa
Boquilla
Búfalo
Mohovano
El Papal
Navojoa
Milpillas
Batopilas
Toquivo
Gral Carlos
Pacheco
San Pablo
Balleza
El Dorado
Jiménez
Villa López
Mapimis
Yávaros
Bacabache
Alamos
Baca
Choix
Yecorato
Guachochic
Santa
Bárbara
Rellano
Carrillo
El Fuerte
San Simón
San Juan
Nepomuceno
El Vergel
Villa de
Orestes
Guadalupe
de Bahues
Ceballos
Yermo
Tlahualilo
de Zaragoza
El Anuajil
San Blas
San José
de Gracia
Ocorini
Guadalupe
y Calvo
La Catedral
Las Nieves
San Fermín
Los Mochis
Topolobampo
Guasave
Naranjo
Bacubirito
Aserradero
Yerbitas
Guanaceví
San Bernardo
Indé
La Zarca
Bermejillo
San Rafael
Cantabr
Isla de San Ignacio
Las Glorias
Buenavista
Guamuchil
Bajios
de Agua Blanca
San José
de la Boca
Ciénega
de Escobar
El Palmito
Ciudad Lerdo
Gómez Palacio
Torreón
Tepanita
Santiago
de los Caballeros
Topia
Tepehuanes
El Casco
Rodeo
Viesca
Isla Altamura
Baturi
Pericos
Presa
Adolfo López
Mateos
El Varejonal
La Templada
de Derrume
Las Herreras
Morelos
Peñon
Blanco
Cuencamé
Yerbanis
Benito
Juárez
Santa Cruz
del Oregano
Culiacancito
Tamazula
Santiago
Papasquiaro
Nuevo Ideal
Francisco
I Madero
Guadalupe
Victoria
Santa
Clara
La Mancha
Bajio de
Ahuichila
Culiacán
Comedero
DURANGO
La Alameda
Canatlán
San Juan
del Río
Santa Cruz
del Oregano
Juan
Aldama
Los Puentes
Altata
Quila
Santa Cruz
Huajuapan
Venustiano
Carranza
Guadalupe
Victoria
Flores
Gracia
El Dorado
Abuya
Guadalupe
de los Reyes
Otinapa
Vicente
Guerrero
Nombre
de Dios
La Cruz
Santa Rosa
San Ignacio
Tayoltita
El Salto
Bayas
Temascal
Ciudad de
Río Grande
Dimas
Cóyotitán
Durango
Tepuxtla
Regócijo
Palo Gordo
de
Tajicaringa
El Quelite
La Nona
Siqueros
Sierra
de los Frailes
Sombrerete
Mazatlán
Concordia
Durango
Jiménez
de Teul
Fresnillo
Villa Unión
El Walarno
Caimanero
El Rosario

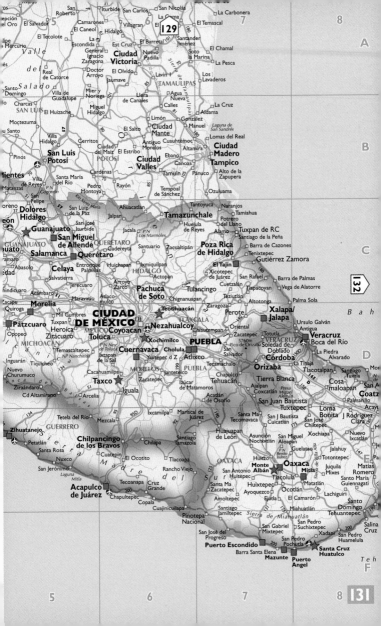

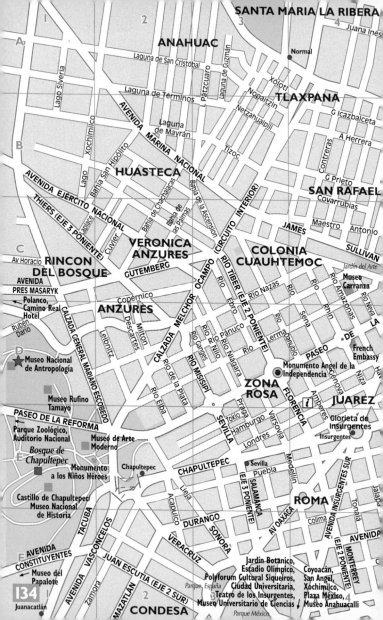

SANTA MARIA LA RIBERA

Juana Inés

ANAHUAC

Laguna de San Cristóbal

Normal

Laguna de Términos

Pátzcuaro

Xólotl

Nopaltzin

TLAXPANA

G Icazbalceta

Laguna de Mayrán

Netzahualpilli

Tizoc

A Herrera

AVENIDA MARINA NACIONAL

Laguna de Mayrán

G Prieto

SAN RAFAEL

HUASTECA

Bahía San Hipólito

Bahía de la Ascensión

Covarrubias

AVENIDA EJERCITO NACIONAL

Laplace

Bahía de Chachalacas

Bahía de las Palmas

CIRCUITO INTERIOR

JAMES

Maestro

Antonio

THIERS (EJE 3 PONIENTE)

Cuvier

SULLIVAN

VERONICA
ANZURES

OCAMPO

COLONIA
CUAUHTEMOC

Jardín del Arte

Av Horacio

RINCON
DEL BOSQUE

GUTEMBERG

MELCHOR

Río Tíber (EJE 2 PONIENTE)

Río Nazas

Museo
Carranza

AVENIDA
PRES MASARYK

Copérnico

Río Ebro

Río Rhin

Río Amazonas

Río Neva

Polanco,
Camino Real
Hotel

CALZADA GENERAL MARIANO ESCOBEDO

ANZURES

Descartes

Milton

CALZADA

Río Pánuco

Río Sena

Rubén Darío

Leibnitz

Río Ganges

RÍO MISSISIPI

Río Nilo

Río de la Plata

Río Nágara

Lerma

Río Danubio

PASEO

DE

LA

French
Embassy

Museo Nacional
de Antropología

Monumento Angel de la
Independencia

Río Elba

ZONA
ROSA

FLORENCIA

Museo Rufino
Tamayo

Amberes

Génova

Niza

JUAREZ

PASEO DE LA REFORMA

i

Parque Zoológico,
Auditorio Nacional

Museo de Arte
Moderno

SEVILLA

Tokio

Praga

Hamburgo

Varsovia

Glorieta de
Insurgentes

Bosque de
Chapultepec

Chapultepec

Londres

Insurgentes

Monumento
a los Niños Héroes

CHAPULTEPEC
(EJE 3 PONIENTE)

Sevilla

Medellín

Castillo de Chapultepec
Museo Nacional
de Historia

TACUBA

Lieja

Acapulco

SALAMANCA
(EJE 3 PONIENTE)

Puebla

ROMA

DURANGO

SONORA

AV OAXACA

Colima

Tonalá

AVENIDA
CONSTITUYENTES

AVENIDA VASCONCELOS

JUAN ESCUTIA (EJE 2 SUR)

VERACRUZ

AVENIDA INSURGENTES SUR

AVENIDA INSURGENTES SUR

MONTERREY
(EJE 2 PONIENTE)

Museo del
Papalote

Zamora

MAZATLAN

Parque España

Jardín Botánico,
Estadio Olímpico,
Polyforum Cultural Siqueiros,
Ciudad Universitaria,
Teatro de los Insurgentes,
Museo Universitario de Ciencias

Coyoacán,
San Ángel,
Xochimilco,
Plaza México,
Museo Anahuacalli

Juanacatlán

CONDESA

Parque México

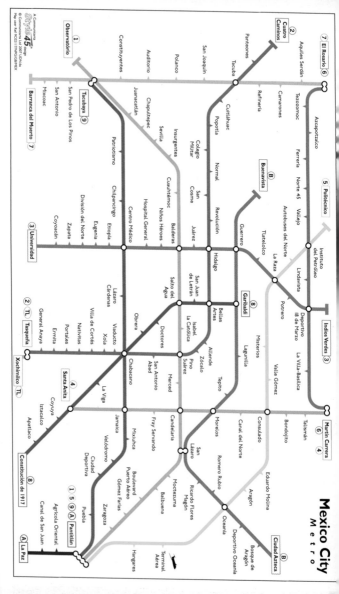

Mexico City
M e t r o

Notes

Notes

Notes

Notes

Notes

Notes

Notes

Notes